My Adventure

THE MAKING OF

An electronics engineer by training, Suresh Jindal got interested in cinema while studying at the University of California, Los Angeles, US, in the late 1960s. He was among the producers who made possible the dreams of film-makers working outside the mainstream. He has produced films that are considered milestones in Indian arthouse cinema, including *Rajnigandha, Shatranj Ke Khilari, Gandhi* and *Katha*. He is a recipient of the Chevalier des Ordre des Arts et des Lettres given by the French government.

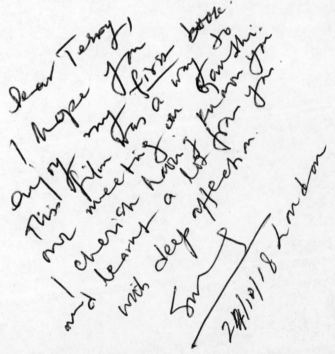

Dear Terry,

I hope you enjoy my first book. This film has a way to our meeting on Gandhi. I cherish having known you and learnt a lot from you.

with deep affection

Suresh

24/10/18 London

My Adventures with Satyajit Ray

THE MAKING OF *SHATRANJ KE KHILARI*

Suresh Jindal

With an Introduction by
Andrew Robinson

HarperCollins *Publishers* India

First published in India in 2017 by
HarperCollins *Publishers*

Copyright © Suresh Jindal 2017

P-ISBN: 978-93-5277-102-8
E-ISBN: 978-93-5277-103-5

2 4 6 8 10 9 7 5 3 1

HarperCollins *Publishers*

A-75, Sector 57, Noida, Uttar Pradesh 201301, India
1 London Bridge Street, London, SE1 9GF, United Kingdom
2 Bloor Street East, Toronto, Ontario M4W 1A8, Canada
Lvl 13, 201 Elizabeth Street (PO Box A565, NSW, 1235),
Sydney NSW 2000, Australia
195 Broadway, New York, NY 10007, USA

Typeset in 12/15 Arno Pro at
SÜRYA, New Delhi

Printed and bound at
Thomson Press (India) Ltd

Dedicated to my late parents,
who taught me to revere creativity and creators

Contents

Contents

Foreword

Impossible Not to Open the Door

I heard about Satyajit Ray for the first time from Luis Buñuel. He had seen *Pather Panchali* (*Song of the Road*, 1955) at Cannes and told me: 'You must see this film, and see it several times [he did insist]. The director is a great one.'

I saw *Pather Panchali*, and I saw it several times, following Buñuel's instructions. Then I watched Ray's other films, one by one, and loved all of them. *Jalsaghar* (*The Music Room*, 1958) is among my all-time favourites. I have seen it six or seven times (and I'll see it again and again).

I was lucky enough to meet Satyajit in Calcutta in 1982. I was travelling through India with Peter Brook, looking for any help, any indication or suggestion that could come to our rescue, for we were working on our stage adaptation of *The Mahabharata*.

Satyajit was nice enough to receive us in his office several times and give us priceless advice. He even told us that for a long time he had himself dreamed of making a film based on the great Indian epic. But the project would have been expensive and would have to be shot in English, preferably with American actors.[1] 'I gave up, because I couldn't imagine Kirk Douglas playing Arjuna,' Ray said with a smile.

We met again several times in Calcutta in the following years. I remember sitting next to him during the screening of one of his last films, *Shakha Proshakha* (*Branches of the Tree*, 1990). As always, I felt his strong presence. When I watched his unforgettable last declaration the day he received the Academy's Honorary Award for Lifetime Achievement on television in Paris, tears welled up in my eyes. I knew I would never see him again. A great artist, and a great man, was leaving us. And he was aware of it.

When it comes to Suresh, it's strange, but I don't remember when I first met him; I just know that we are friends. We met several times in India, maybe thirty years ago, but also in Paris and—strangely enough—in Mexico. We had long conversations, and together we even cautiously explored the jungle near Palenque in the Maya country. Suresh kept pretending that his

---

1. Since this kind of film required a large budget, it would have been necessary to cast stars, as they would bring in the distribution.

light Indian sandals were the best possible shoes for walking in an unexplored forest, which, to this day, I doubt.

One day he sent me the manuscript of this book, containing the letters exchanged between Satyajit Ray and himself regarding the movie he had produced, *Shatranj Ke Khilari* (*The Chess Players*, 1977), which is set in Lucknow in the nineteenth century, precisely in 1856. And I was seduced at once, because I had never read anything like it before: the story of the making of a film, step by step, from beginning to end. The relations between a film director and a producer are usually secretive. They can sometimes be treacherous, even violent. And they remain a mystery to the crew and, consequently, to the audience.

While reading Suresh's book (and looking at the pictures and documents it contains), we discover what's generally hidden. It's like walking into an adventure novel, where you penetrate another jungle full of delusions and dangers, but with the best possible guides. I guess even if we don't belong to the world of cinema (and we don't need to in order to enjoy this book), we partake of the desires, the worries, the hesitations, the difficulties and also the joys these two men faced along the way in making a great film.

A legend (Suresh regards Ray as 'a magnificent human specimen', a 'towering personality') is coming to visit us,

to share his dreams with us, as if we were part of his team;
I would even say, as part of his family.

And it's impossible not to open the door and let him
in.

JEAN-CLAUDE CARRIÈRE

Introduction

'Suresh, every film is like an adventure!'[1]—Satyajit Ray
(while researching *Shatranj Ke Khilari* in Lucknow)

Shatranj Ke Khilari (*The Chess Players*), completed in 1977, was the first adult film about the British Raj in India. Today, after *Gandhi, Heat and Dust, The Jewel in the Crown, A Passage to India, Lagaan* and many other films, Satyajit Ray's film remains by far the most sophisticated portrayal of this particular clash of cultures. No other director—British, Indian or otherwise—is likely to better it. As V.S. Naipaul remarked, 'It is like a Shakespeare scene. Only 300 words are spoken but goodness!—terrific things happen.'[2]

---

1. See p. 50.

2. Interview with V.S. Naipaul in 1987, quoted in Andrew Robinson, *Satyajit Ray: The Inner Eye*, 2nd edn, London: I.B. Tauris, 2004, p. 246.

Ray had known Premchand's short story 'Shatranj Ke Khilari' for more than thirty years before he attempted to make a screenplay out of it, after meeting the young producer Suresh Jindal in 1974. Although it had first appeared in print in Hindi in the mid-1920s, Ray read it in English translation in the early 1940s as an art student at Rabindranath Tagore's university in Bengal and was immediately drawn to it for several reasons.

Lucknow, the setting of the story, is one of the most resonant cities in India. Satyajit took holidays there in the late 1920s and 1930s from the age of about eight, staying at first in the house of an uncle, later with other relatives. The uncle, a barrister called Atulprasad Sen, was the most famous Bengali composer of songs after Tagore. His house hummed with music of every kind, and his guests displayed polished manners to match; they included the greatest north Indian classical musician of modern times, Ustad Allauddin Khan (the father of Ali Akbar Khan and the guru of Ravi Shankar). The young Ray listened to him playing the piano and violin, and took in the atmosphere of courtly refinement that was so characteristic of Lucknow. He was also taken to see all the sights that had made Lucknow known as the 'Paris of the East' and the 'Babylon of India' a century before: the great mosque Bara Imambara with its notorious Bhulbhulaiya Maze, the Dilkusha Garden and the remains of the palaces of the Kings of Awadh (Oudh). Nearby he saw the shell of the British Residency, with the marks of cannonballs still visible on its walls and a marble plaque commemorating the spot where Sir Henry Lawrence had fallen during the Indian Mutiny/Uprising of 1857. Even today these places have a peculiar elegiac aura. The brief allusions to the city and that period in its history in Premchand's story conjured up a host of images and sensations in the twenty-year-old Ray's mind.

By then he was also keenly interested in chess. Over the next ten years or so this became an addiction—the main bond (along with Western classical music) between him and his first English friend, Norman Clare, an RAF serviceman with time on his hands in Calcutta in 1944-46. After this friend was demobbed, Ray found himself without a partner and took to playing solitaire chess. Over the next few years he became engrossed in it and bought books on chess, which he would soon decide to sell to raise money to shoot the pilot footage for his first film, *Pather Panchali*. His passion for chess disappeared only with the onset of a greater passion: film-making.

That came around 1951, after his return to Calcutta from his first visit to Britain. Nearly a quarter of a century passed before Ray tackled the story he had admired as a student. His reluctance was principally due to his doubts about writing a screenplay and working with actors in a language—Urdu, the court language of Lucknow (which is very similar to Hindi, the language of Premchand's story)—that was not his own. So rich, subtle and lifelike is Ray's usual film dialogue—as Naipaul appreciated from just the portions of *The Chess Players* in English—so nuanced his direction of actors that he feared to work in a language other than Bengali or perhaps English. It was his affection for the story, his discovery of able Urdu collaborators and his awareness of a pool of talented Urdu-speaking actors in Bombay (rather than his usual Calcutta) which eventually gave him confidence. For the first time—excepting his science-fiction project, *The Alien*, and his documentaries—Ray wrote a screenplay in English, which was subsequently translated into Urdu. During production, he spoke English to his producer Jindal, the actors and his Urdu collaborators. Although his Hindi was serviceable, Ray characteristically avoided speaking in Hindi. 'He doesn't like to do anything unless he's really good at it,' Shama Zaidi, his chief collaborator in the writing of the screenplay, remarked.

Her role in the film began early on, about two years before Ray completed the first draft of the screenplay in June 1976. Ray's art director Bansi Chandragupta introduced Zaidi to Ray in 1974. He was just beginning to get to grips with his research for the film—which makes it one of the longest pre-production periods of any Ray film (during which he made another film, *Jana Aranya* [*The Middle Man*]). It is not hard to see why: not only had Ray taken on the re-creation of an entire culture that was not his own, he was also having to confront his own ambivalence towards the British Raj and, in particular, the contradictions of King Wajid Ali Shah, one of the most bizarre monarchs in a land of eccentric rulers.

Since Ray has regularly been condemned for failing to make his own attitude to the Indian and British sides clear in *Shatranj Ke Khilari*—notably in a long attack on the film for accepting the British view of Wajid Ali Shah as being 'effete and effeminate',[3] published in the *Illustrated Weekly of India*, to which Ray responded at length—it is worth detailing the principal sources he consulted in his research in India and, later, in the India Office Library in London. Some of them pop up in his wonderfully detailed and revealing letters to Suresh Jindal that form the spine of *My Adventures with Satyajit Ray*, a compellingly readable, honest and touching memoir of a great artist in the throes of creation. 'Ray was a tireless and outstanding researcher,'[4] notes Jindal. 'Just accompanying him to his meetings with scholars, academicians, experts and specialists in music, art, architecture and military history was an amazing experience and taught me a great deal.'

Ray listed his sources in his reply to the attack as follows, adding his own comments on their significance,

3. Rajbans Khanna, 'Ray's Wajid Ali Shah', the *Illustrated Weekly of India*, Bombay, 22 October 1978, p. 49.

4. See p. 47.

which are reproduced here along with my own remarks in square brackets:

1. *Blue Book on Oude*.[5] This is the official British dossier on the Annexation. It contains, among other things, a verbatim account of Outram's last interview with Wajid, and describes Wajid's taking off his turban and handing it to Outram as a parting gesture.

2. Abdul Halim Sharar's *Guzeshta Lucknow* (translated into English by E.S. Harcourt and Fakhir Hussain as *Lucknow: The Last Phase of an Oriental Culture*). Sharar was born three years after Wajid's deposition [in 1856]. His father worked in the Secretariat of Wajid's court and joined Wajid [in exile in Calcutta] in 1862. Sharar went and joined his father seven years later. Introducing the book, the translators say: 'The work has long been recognised by Indo-Islamic scholars as a primary source of great value, a unique document both alive and authentic in every detail.' Sharar provided most of the socio-cultural details, as well as a fairly extended portrait of Wajid, both in his Lucknow and

5. Satyajit Ray, 'My Wajid Ali Shah is not "Effete and Effeminate"!', the *Illustrated Weekly of India*, Bombay, 31 December 1978, p. 50.

his Calcutta periods. [Luckily for Ray this wonderful book appeared in English just in time to be of use to him.]

3. The Indian histories of Mill and Beveridge, both critical of the Annexation.

4. Two histories of the Mutiny (by Ball and by Kaye).

5. *The Letters of Lord Dalhousie*. One of these letters provided the information that Outram grumbled about the new treaty and apprehended that Wajid would refuse to sign it. Dalhousie ascribes this attitude to indigestion [an idea that Ray has Outram specifically reject when talking to Dr Fayrer in the film].

6. *The Reminiscences of Sir Alexander Fayrer*. Fayrer was the Resident Surgeon, Honorary Assistant Resident and Postmaster of Lucknow at the time of the takeover.

7. Two biographies of Outram (by Trotter and by Goldschmid).

8. The diaries and letters of Emily Eden, Fanny Eden, Bishop Heber and Fanny Parkes.

9. *The Indian Mutiny Diary* by Howard Russell. Russell came to India as the correspondent of the *Times*. He was on the spot when the British troops ransacked the Kaiserbagh Palace. He

gives the only detailed description of the interior of the palace that I have come across.

10. The young Wajid's personal diary *Mahal Khana Shahi*. This turned out to be an unending account of his amours. [Some think it spurious, but Shama Zaidi did not.]

11. The text of Wajid Ali Shah's *Rahas* [the play he wrote about Krishna that he briefly performs at the beginning of the film].

12. Mrs Meer Hasan Ali's *On the Mussulmans of India* (1832). This was found useful for its details of life in the zenana.

13. *Umrao Jan Ada* (translated into English as *A Courtesan of Lucknow*). This gives a fascinating and authentic picture of Lucknow in Wajid's time.

14. All English and Bengali newspapers and journals of the period preserved in the National Library [in Calcutta].

15. I was also in close touch throughout with Professor Kaukabh of Aligarh University. Professor Kaukabh happens to be a great-grandson of Wajid Ali Shah and is considered to be one of the best authorities in India on Wajid.

In trying to assimilate this array of historical and cultural information with Premchand's story to make a screenplay,

Ray faced certain formidable difficulties. First came the widespread ignorance of the facts of the relationship between Britain and Awadh in the century leading up to the Annexation—in India as much as elsewhere—to which the film's ten-minute prologue seemed the only solution. Second, there was the fact that chess is not inherently dramatic on screen. Third was the need to portray the king sympathetically. Finally, an overall tone had to be found that was in harmony with the pleasure-loving decadence of Lucknow, without seeming to condone it.

The third of these difficulties almost persuaded Ray to abandon the film. He felt a strong, Outram-like aversion for Wajid Ali Shah, the more he knew about his debauches. Jindal, Zaidi and the actor Saeed Jaffrey at one time received letters from him declaring his doubts about whether he could portray the king successfully. When Zaidi wrote to Ray offering to translate Wajid's diary (in which he very explicitly describes his sex life from the age of eight) and his letters from Calcutta to his wife in Lucknow, Ray replied, Shama recalled with amusement, 'Don't tell me all this because then I'll dislike him even more.'[6]

It was Wajid's genuine musical gifts that reconciled Ray to the rest of the king's character. As depicted in

6. Andrew Robinson, *Satyajit Ray: The Inner Eye*, 2nd edn, London: I.B. Tauris, 2004, p. 242.

the film's screenplay, the king was a ruler capable of admonishing his tearful prime minister (whom he had first come to know at the house of a courtesan) by saying: 'Nothing but poetry and music should bring tears to a man's eyes.' One is reminded perhaps of another Ray protagonist—the fossilized nobleman-aesthete in *Jalsaghar* (*The Music Room*), who lives only for music. As Ray said, 'The fact that the king was a great patron of music was one redeeming feature about him. But that came after long months of study, of the nawabs, of Lucknow and everything.'[7]

This became the key that unlocked the character of Outram, too. Among the copious extracts from the sources Ray consulted that are carefully noted down in his bulky shooting notebooks for *Shatranj Ke Khilari*, one comes across this character sketch of Outram with quotes from Goldschmid's biography:

1. Refused to benefit from conquest of Sind [in which campaign Outram had been in command in 1843].
2. Disliked pettifogging ceremony.
3. 'his manner natural and gracious; his speech is marked by a slight hesitation when choosing a word, but it is singularly correct and forcible; and his smile is very genial and sympathetic.'

7. Andrew Robinson, *Satyajit Ray: The Inner Eye*, 2nd edn, London: I.B. Tauris, 2004, p. 242–3.

4. 'His quaint humour'; a good anecdotist.
5. 'he greatly appreciated music of a touching character. Sacred music, always his preference.'

From this description, and knowing the universal dislike of Indian music by the British, one can easily imagine Outram failing signally to comprehend Wajid Ali Shah's—'our fat King's'—gifts as a composer, whilst seeing only too plainly his faults as a ruler. Indian 'impracticality' and Indian love of the inessential—as Outram sees it—baffle and irritate him as they have baffled and irritated the West from the beginning of its encounter with India. But Outram also finds Wajid Ali Shah intriguing. The scene in which he interrogates his Urdu-speaking aide-de-camp, Captain Weston, about the king's doings demonstrates Ray's insight into the nature of cultural friction with exquisite skill, suggesting clearly (but never explicitly) the intimate links between nationalism, racialism and lack of imagination.

In Outram's utilitarian superior Lord Dalhousie, the Governor-General in Calcutta, the hauteur is palpable. The confident, mocking tone of Dalhousie's letters suggested to Ray not only the ironic tone of the film but also, quite directly, the sequence of cartoons in the prologue of the film explaining how the British steadily deprived the rulers of Lucknow of money, land and power while preserving their formal status. Dalhousie was responsible for the annexation of several Indian states before Awadh. In one of his letters—quoted in the film—he refers to Wajid Ali Shah sardonically as 'the wretch in Lucknow'[8] and to Awadh as 'a cherry which will drop into our mouths some day'. Ray immediately decided to depict this literally in the film by showing a cartoon English sahib knocking the crowns off cherries and popping them into his mouth. Although the cartoons are brasher than one would like—one of the few slightly false notes in the film—they are an imaginative and amusing expression of the lack of imagination with which the East India Company generally treated the Indians it ruled: like pawns to be manipulated in a game of chess.

Ray counterpoints this lack with the very different failings of the two chess players, so wrapped up in their games that they barely understand the political game being played with their futures. It took him months of pondering to satisfy himself that such a counterpoint would work on screen. The obstacle, as he told Jindal in an almost despairing letter in April 1976, is that 'the moment you got down to the business of showing the [chess] game, silence and inaction would descend upon the screen—with what consequences you may well imagine'.[9] To Jaffrey he wrote in May: 'If it had been

8. James Dalhousie, *Private Letters of the Marquess of Dalhousie*, edited by J.G.A. Baird, Edinburgh: William Blackwood, 1910, p. 169.

9. See p. 55.

gambling, there would have been no problem. But the beauty of the story lies in the parallel that Premchand draws between the game and the moves of the crafty Raj leading to the "capture" of the king.'[10]

His solution calls to mind two of Ray's earlier films about obsession: *Jalsaghar* (*The Music Room*) and *Devi* (*The Goddess*). In each case, he stresses the human element, without ever losing sight of the object of obsession. Just as it is not essential to be familiar with Indian classical singing or Kali worship (though it is a big advantage with *Devi*) when watching these films, one need have no knowledge of chess to appreciate *Shatranj Ke Khilari*.

However, Ray was no doubt greatly assisted by his former passion for the game in building on Premchand's basic conceit. Deftly, he found a hundred ways on screen to express Meer's and Mirza's utter absorption in their private world, enriching his theme so naturally and imperceptibly that its final impact defies analysis. All of his best films have been like this: *Pather Panchali, The Postmaster, Charulata, Aranyer Din Ratri* (*Days and Nights in the Forest*), *Asani Sanket* (*Distant Thunder*), to name some of them. He had grasped the importance of this way of constructing a film as far back as 1950 after watching Vittorio de Sica's *The Bicycle Thief* and a hundred

10. Andrew Robinson, *Satyajit Ray: The Inner Eye*, 2nd edn, London: I.B. Tauris, 2004, p. 245.

other films in London, when he wrote to his friend Bansi Chandragupta in Calcutta (then assisting Eugene Lourié in Jean Renoir's *The River*), as follows:

> The entire conventional approach (as exemplified by even the best American and British films) is wrong. Because the conventional approach tells you that the best way to tell a story is to leave out all except those elements which are directly related to the story, while the master's work clearly indicates that if your theme is strong and simple, then you can include a hundred little apparently irrelevant details which, instead of obscuring the theme, only help to intensify it by contrast, and in addition create the illusion of actuality better.[11]

Ray's theme in *Shatranj Ke Khilari* is strong and simple—that the non-involvement of India's ruling classes assisted a small number of British in their takeover of India—but the way he expresses the theme is oblique and complex. It is not at first apparent, for example, what Mirza's ignorance of his wife's dissatisfaction with him may have to do with Outram's intention to annex Awadh; but by the end the link is clear, when Mirza's cuckolded friend

---

11. Marie Seton, *Satyajit Ray: Portrait of a Director*, 2nd edn, London: Dobson, 1978, p. 165.

Meer remarks to him with comic pathos in their village hideaway: 'We can't even cope with our wives, so how we can cope with the Company's army?' This is the moment in the film where Ray intends the two interwoven stories to become one, the moment of truth where all the pieces in the puzzle fall magically into place. Rather than the shattering revelation of the ending of *Charulata*—where Bhupati suddenly perceives his complete failure to understand his wife—the ending of *Shatranj Ke Khilari* recalls Ashim's deflation by Aparna at the end of *Aranyer Din Ratri*. Though painful, it is also funny, made bearable for Meer and Mirza by their continuing affection for each other.

Neither of these films has much story as such. Yet, the entire Indo-Muslim culture of Lucknow is suggested in *Shatranj Ke Khilari*, rather as Jean Renoir suggests French bourgeois society between the wars in *La Règle du Jeu*. Music and dance figure prominently, since it is important for us to grasp their highly regarded position in Wajid Ali Shah's world. His decision finally to renounce his throne without a fight is communicated to his courtiers not through mere words but through a musical couplet: a thumri of the kind made famous by Wajid, in fact his most famous thumri in India today (of which Ray knew a variation as a boy in Calcutta):

Jab chhorh chaley Lakhnau nagari
Kaho haal adam par kya guzeri...

Which may be roughly translated as:

> When we left Lucknow,
> See what befell us…

On the printed page in English translation it may lack impact, but when sung by Amjad Khan in a hesitant voice, husky with emotion, it is moving.

In the later stages of making and releasing *Shatranj Ke Khilari*—so frankly recounted by Jindal, including his near-withdrawal from the film after a painful dispute with Ray—Ray must sometimes have felt the thumri could apply to him too:

> When I left Bengal,
> See what befell me…

After Herculean efforts to film the East India Company troops arriving in Lucknow—in the midsummer heat of Jaipur, because only there could the necessary Indian army horses be made available—Ray managed to get the film finished by September 1977. But when it was shown to prospective Indian distributors, five of them withdrew their support, apparently dissatisfied with the classical nature of the film's songs and dances and its use of high-flown Urdu: they had obviously been anticipating more razzmatazz. 'Mr Ray has made the film for a foreign audience'[12] was the comment Ray passed on to Jaffrey rather gloomily in a letter at the end of October. But he knew that the film had also received an excellent response at a screening in Bombay. So good, rumour has it that it made some of the big guns in the Bombay film industry conspire to prevent the film from getting a proper release in India. The language of *Shatranj Ke Khilari* being Hindi/Urdu, rather than Ray's usual Bengali, and the presence of Bombay stars (Amjad Khan and Sanjeev Kumar in particular) may have provoked fears of their own song-and-dance products being undermined. In India, the film 'was off to a rough start in terms of release and general acceptance',[13] writes Jindal, remembering his own frustrations and despondency at this time.

Most Indians probably expected a more full-blooded treatment of the Raj in the manner of Richard Attenborough's (later) *Gandhi*; Ray's restraint and irony towards both sides did not please them. The hostile critic in the *Illustrated Weekly* complained that the film gave no sense of the way that discontent over the 1856 Annexation helped to bring about the 1857 Uprising. Rajbans Khanna wrote: 'Study the records of this period and you realise how glaring is Satyajit's failure in giving us a picture of a placid and uneventful Lucknow in which his characters move about like lifeless dummies in an

---

12. Andrew Robinson, *Satyajit Ray: The Inner Eye*, 2nd edn, London: I.B. Tauris, 2004, p. 250.

13. See p. 135.

empty shadowplay.'[14]

Abroad, the film had a warm reception, though not by any means as warm as for much of Ray's earlier work. Probably the most perceptive comment came from Tim Radford in the *Guardian*: 'Satyajit Ray seems to be able to achieve more and more with less and less.'[15] Most Western critics, however, found the film slow, and many found it mannered; also, like most Indians, too bloodless for their taste. Vincent Canby in the *New York Times* was perhaps typical in writing that, 'Ray's not outraged. Sometimes he's amused; most often he's meditative, and unless you respond to this mood, the movie is so overly polite that you may want to shout a rude word.'[16]

Neither East nor West seemed quite satisfied with *Shatranj Ke Khilari*. Both wanted Ray to have painted his canvas in bolder colours. Yet, as he pointed out at the time,

> the condemnation *is* there, ultimately, but the process of arriving at it is different. I was portraying two negative forces, feudalism and

14. Rajbans Khanna, 'Ray's Wajid Ali Shah', the *Illustrated Weekly of India*, Bombay, 22 October 1978, p. 53.

15. Tim Radford, 'A Kingdom in Pawn', *Guardian*, London, 18 January 1979.

16. Vincent Canby, 'Ray Satirizes Indian Nobility', the *New York Times*, New York, 17 May 1978.

colonialism. You had to condemn both Wajid and Dalhousie. This was the challenge. I wanted to make this condemnation interesting by bringing in certain plus points of both sides. You have to read this film between the lines.[17]

Most of Ray's films—as he quietly but frankly observed on a number of occasions—can be fully appreciated only by someone with insight into Indian *and* Western culture. 'I'm thankful for the fact that ... I'm familiar with both cultures and it gives me a very much stronger footing as a film-maker,' Ray told me in 1982 when I was researching his biography.[18] *Shatranj Ke Khilari* undoubtedly gains in meaning if one studies the history and forms of artistic expression of the Mughals and their successors in Lucknow, as well as the attitude to those successors epitomized by General Outram when he lambasts Wajid as 'a frivolous, irresponsible, worthless king'. If Naipaul, a Nobel laureate and one of the great writers of our time, is right in comparing Ray with Shakespeare, one may safely predict that people will still be watching this unique film and discovering new things in it, for very many years to come.

ANDREW ROBINSON

17. Andrew Robinson, *Satyajit Ray: The Inner Eye*, 2nd edn, London: I.B. Tauris, 2004, p. 251.

18. Andrew Robinson, *Satyajit Ray: The Inner Eye*, 2nd edn, London: I.B. Tauris, 2004, p. 240.

1

The Meeting

♟♟♟♟♟♟

My first film, *Rajnigandha*, based on the story 'Yehi Sach Hai' by Mannu Bhandari, turned out to be the sleeper hit of 1974. Since almost everyone involved with the project was new to Hindi cinema—this was years before the industry would come to be known as Bollywood—along with the euphoria of having made it in the film industry, I was confused about what project to undertake next.

Later that year, the critically acclaimed Bengali film-maker Satyajit Ray, recognized as an icon of world cinema, delivered the convocation address at the Film and Television Institute of India (FTII), Pune, the premier film school of the country. He was addressing eager young graduates, raring to make 'art for art's sake', prepared to alienate audiences in their quest for expression. But in his speech, he gently urged them not to have contempt for the audience because 'a film-maker who blames the audience for not liking his films is akin to a cook blaming the diner for not liking a badly cooked fish'. Reading his speech, and this quote in particular, in the newspaper the next day and realizing how important the audience was to him, I got the feeling that he might finally be ready to make a film for a larger audience than his past films had been able to attract.

Maybe he was now open to making a movie in a language other than his mother tongue, Bengali. Perhaps Hindi, or English?

I knew he had already refused offers by such stalwarts as Raj Kapoor, S.S. Vasan and Tarachand Barjatya to make a film in Hindi; perhaps it was the audacity of youth, sudden success and a deep longing just to be with this great man that nurtured such fantasies in me. When I was still an engineering student abroad, at the University of California, Los Angeles (UCLA), it was the genius of his films, among those of other master film-makers, that awakened me to the beauty of cinema. As far back as I can remember, I had hoped one day to be able to pay my respects in person to this extraordinary man. And beyond that lay the inexpressible and impossible dream of working with him in some capacity some day.

~

It was a Saturday afternoon in September 1974 at the Anands' beach flat in Juhu, Bombay. The brothers—actor–director Tinnu and producer Bittu—and I were enjoying our usual round of beers before a late lunch, feeling quite mellow. With my own family residing in New Delhi, the Anands were my family in Bombay, and their love and warmth played an integral part in my success. Tinnu had been Ray's assistant for five years and he regaled me with anecdotes about his time working with him.

'Tinnu, I have a strong feeling that Manik-da will do a film in Hindi soon,' I blurted out, voicing my hopes out loud for the first time.

'I think so too, buddy,' he replied.

It was not the answer I expected.

'Are you serious?' I asked, incredulous.

'I really feel it.' Tinnu's face seemed to confirm his words.

For a second I let his statement sink in ... then in a flash of excitement I exploded, 'So let's call him and go meet him!'

Within minutes we had booked a call to Calcutta through the operator; there was no long-distance direct-dial in those days. While waiting for the call to go through, Tinnu beseeched me, 'Promise me that if he still doesn't want to do a film in Hindi or in English, you'll do one in Bengali with him?'

'I've made a lot of money lately. I don't need another blockbuster right now. All I want is to work with the great man … in *any* language. Sure, I'll do it in Bengali!'

After what felt like an eternity the call went through. I stared at Tinnu while he conversed with Ray in Bengali—a language I don't speak or understand. I could hardly wait for the call to be over to hear the verdict. When he finally put the receiver down I practically yelled, 'Will he see us?'

'He says we can go see him and talk.'

I savoured his words while grinning widely at Tinnu, who smiled back and said, 'Better book us on the earliest flight you can get to Calcutta.'

~

In Calcutta, we checked into the Grand Hotel and Tinnu left to meet Ray by himself first, as was instructed. By the time he returned, I was overwhelmed by apprehension and hope.

'Is it okay? Will he see me?' I enquired.

'We can meet him at 10 a.m. tomorrow.'

I was delighted by the dream-come-true quality of these words, but quickly focused on more practical matters. 'Did he say yes to a Hindi or an English film?'

Tinnu shrugged and remained silent. He obviously didn't want to disclose Ray's decision. Usually, I like this about Tinnu very much—the way he can clam up totally.

If anybody wants to deposit secrets that are not to be revealed, he is their man. But not today. I was frustrated. Realizing that, he tried to soothe me.

'You just speak to Manik-da the way you spoke to me, and I'm sure everything will work out fine.'

Night fell. A night of dread and elation. The clattering of hope and despair. Legends about him danced in my mind: Renaissance man, one of the top storywriters of our time, creative director of an advertising agency with two fonts named after him (Ray Roman and Ray Bizarre), scriptwriter, brilliant director, camera operator, production and graphic designer, music director. This man whose movies I used to watch in small art theatres around UCLA had aroused such deep pride and joy in me, that India could produce masterpieces of world cinema and that one of the world's greatest film-makers was someone from my own country.

To be around him would be like completing an entire curriculum in cinema, better than any offered across the globe. I was just a rookie, only one film old, and I wanted to learn film-making from the best. My effrontery amazed and scared me. But my determination to fulfil my secret dream prevailed.

I could hardly sleep that night.

~

The next morning, we were early for our appointment. It was sweltering and by the time we had trudged up the grand staircase in a majestic colonial building to the ten-foot-high white door to Ray's second-floor flat, we were panting and sweating. While Tinnu rang the doorbell, I slid behind him to be as unobtrusive as possible, because it was well-known that Ray personally opened the door for his visitors.

Suddenly, a magnificent human specimen, tall with a bright face opened the door. A voice whose fame had already become legendary greeted us, and now, as it was directed at us, its impact hit me with delightful force. In his imposing, rich, but incredibly warm and friendly, baritone, he invited us to enter.

I was still a few months shy of my thirty-third birthday; he was fifty-seven years old. I was 5'6" tall and he was 6'2", a veritable giant by Indian standards. I was from a well-to-do, non-intellectual, conservative, vegetarian Jain–Bania family from Punjab. Our caste as traders and industrialists was—and still is—looked down upon as being the Jews of India; and Punjabis have often been told that the only culture we have is agriculture. Whereas Ray was from a distinguished family of Bengal—half a continent away from my home—that was aristocratic, highly accomplished both academically and artistically and progressive; his grandfather was among the early leaders of the socio-religious Hindu reform movement, the Brahmo Samaj. I had lived in half a dozen countries; he had never lived anywhere but in Calcutta. I was a young, hot-headed Indian engineer trained in the US, radicalized by American counterculture and the movements of the 1960s, now turned film-maker. He was a legend, a calm, accomplished master of his craft.

As we followed him into the flat, I reflected on my good fortune in having lived through some of the landmark developments of our time and having been taught by some of the most amazing minds. Life in the US in the 1960s was among the headiest experiences of the twentieth century: the space race to the moon, the computer explosion, freedom rides against segregation in the south, flower power, psychedelic drugs, love-ins, environmental protection, gay liberation, hippies, Jesus freaks, brilliant college professors who were also Nobel Prize winners, tripped-out rock stars, raving John Birchers and ranting doomsday evangelists. The Kennedys, Martin Luther King, the Beatles, Maharishi Mahesh Yogi, Ravi Shankar and J. Krishnamurti. Zen Buddhism freshly imported to the West, Timothy Leary and the acid heads, gun-toting Black Panthers, tattooed Hell's Angels, anti–Vietnam War demonstrations—all intermingled in an unending dervish-like dance during my ten years abroad. Our age was one of innovative and creative ideas—one characterized by a desire to acquire wisdom, to save the world from atomic devastation, to attain truth, beauty, freedom, love and self-respect. Our ideal leaders were liberal humanists rather than juntas of generals, hedonistic aristocrats or business tycoons.

~

We followed Satyajit Ray into his famous study, a place where he could be found whenever he was not shooting or on a rare social engagement. It looked like a combination of a Renaissance atelier and an alchemist's lab. The first third of the space we entered was a lobby-cum-library where Ray's collection of rare books was housed, along with some of his awards. The rest of the space was used as a study, research centre, studio, music room, conference room and adda, a colloquial Bengali word meaning a den or hang-out.

He sat down in a far corner on a swivel chair and faced the room. Behind him were two large windows and a cluttered desk with a telephone, which I was told he always answered himself. At hand was an easel with a small table next to it, overflowing with paints and brushes. Facing him, along the bookshelf wall, was a padded armchair where his chief visitor was asked to sit, and where he now indicated I should have a seat. To the right of the armchair was a table and another chair, against the wall to the right a full-size sofa, a piano and a music system in the corner. Along the opposite wall there was another sofa, this one sagging with books, journals, research material, manuscripts and notebooks heaped in disarray, obviously in continuous use. The entire workspace was large enough to accommodate at least ten people.

A production meeting had evidently been going on with Anil Choudhury, Soumendu Roy, Ashok Das and others. His team had been with him from the beginning and was more like family than crew. He later told me that one reason he needed to make a film each year was to keep them employed, since they worked almost exclusively for him.

My film *Rajnigandha* was currently running to packed houses at the Metro cinema in Calcutta, for which Ray and everyone in the room congratulated me. Tea and biscuits were brought in, as I discovered over time they usually were, in endless streams for anybody who visited. After a few more pleasantries, his team left Tinnu and me alone with him.

I felt hot and breathless and perspired even though it was quite cool under the ceiling fan. Rooted to the spot in my armchair I didn't see how I would ever get a word unstuck from my throat: So much was riding on the outcome of the next few minutes.

He turned to me and in English gently asked me for my say.

'Sir, I would like you to make a film in Hindi because I am in the Hindi film industry, or in English, or if not, then in Bengali,' the words tumbled out. As soon as I heard them, I panicked at the disjointed, abrupt and almost rude sentences. *Oh, you've blown it, Suresh! Better get out of here fast before you sink to the floor with embarrassment.*

Then a voice cut through my despairing thoughts, not unlike what the Prophet Moses must have heard while receiving the Ten Commandments from God, and said, 'Actually ... I have been thinking of doing a film in Hindi.'

His reply lifted me out of the darkness that had threatened to devour me just a second ago and thrust me towards a future full of endless possibilities. I looked at him in amazement and infinite gratitude.

'If you come across a story that you like, let me know. If I like it, I will do a screenplay.'

Even though I was just a rookie and dazed by the last few minutes, I *did* know enough about the film industry to realize that when a great director decides to make a film he said he never would, something besides my blathering must have inspired him.

'Sir, might you have a story in mind ... ?'

'Yes, I do. But before I tell you what it is, you must agree not to reveal it to anybody, in case we decide not to do it.'

'Certainly.'

'Also, I must warn you it will be a very expensive film. At least four or five times more expensive than my costliest Bengali film. You may not want to spend so much on my first Hindi film.'

'Yes, sir, I understand. But that's not a problem.'

'The story is called "Shatranj Ke Khilari". It is a short story by Premchand. Do you know it?'

'Not this particular one, but I would like to read it. Is there an English translation?'

'Yes, there is a UNESCO publication that has it. But I will lend you my copy only if you will return it after reading it.'

After one more round of tea and biscuits, I floated out the same way I came in, but this time with a book in hand like a precious talisman. Back on the landing after the great door shut, Tinnu and I grinned at one another in delight and flew down the wide staircase three steps at a time. We rushed back to the Grand and I started devouring the book.

I liked it immensely.

The next day we returned and I told him so. I said I would love to do the story and handed over an envelope, mumbling, 'Sir, this is for you.'

'Baba, what's this?'

'Sir, in the Bombay film industry when a director and producer agree to do a film together, it is customary for the producer to give the director a signing amount.'

'No. I don't work that way. And if we are to work together, you will have to work my way. First, I will write a draft of the screenplay, and if it is satisfactory, we can discuss money.'

I smiled at him, bowed my head in respect and withdrew the envelope. And thus began my professional relationship and a lifelong friendship with Satyajit Ray.

2

Satyajit Ray: A Brief Biography

♟♟♟♟♟♟

Any Indian who can read knows of Satyajit Ray. His name and work are held in high esteem even twenty-five years after his death, despite several decades without a new Ray film and the unavailability of many of his films on video or DVD during his lifetime. His oeuvre continues to exert a strong influence on the collective psyche. This man broke through insurmountable barriers to make movies that are respected and honoured throughout the world.

In cinema circles, along with Japan's Akira Kurosawa, Italy's Federico Fellini, Sweden's Ingmar Bergman, Mexico's Luis Buñuel, Russia's Andrei Tarkovsky, Germany's R.W. Fassbinder, France's Jean Renoir, Jean-Luc Godard and François Truffaut, and America's D.W. Griffith, Alfred Hitchcock, Billy Wilder, Martin Scorsese and Steven Spielberg, Ray is regarded as one of the greatest film-makers of all time.

But sadly, due to the unavailability of his films on video until recently, most people in other parts of the world are not aware of his name or his masterpieces as compared to those of the other great directors.

I cannot take credit for the information provided in this chapter, and everything here has been gleaned from various Ray biographies and from the websites www.satyajitray.org and www.satyajitrayworld.com. Almost anything you might want to know about this great film-maker, as well as the titles of several biographies, can be found there. But a short introduction to Ray and his work here is imperative to understand who it was that I made the film *Shatranj Ke Khilari* with, and how lucky I was to have had this incredible opportunity.

~

Satyajit Ray was born on 2 May 1921 into an intellectual and affluent family in Calcutta. His grandfather Upendrakishore Ray Chaudhuri was a distinguished writer, painter and composer who founded U. Ray and Sons, one of the finest printing presses in the country, as well as a popular Bengali children's magazine called *Sandesh*. His father, Sukumar Ray, also a talented writer, poet and illustrator, studied printing technology in England and joined the family business. He was a frequent contributor to *Sandesh*. With these influences, it isn't hard to see how even as a child Satyajit became fascinated with block-making, printing, illustrating and writing.

Unfortunately, Ray's grandfather had passed away six years before he was born, and his father fell ill the year he was born and died soon after. About three years after his father's death, the family's printing and publishing business folded up, and Satyajit and his mother had to leave their spacious house and move in with relatives, where she taught needlework to supplement the family income. Until the age of eight, his mother homeschooled him and later enrolled him in a government school, where he was an average student. While still at school, Ray became a film buff, regularly reading about Hollywood movies and film stars in magazines. Western classical music became another great interest; he would pick up old records at flea markets and listen to them at home, enraptured by the sounds emanating from the gramophone.

Ray graduated from high school when he was just short of fifteen. His mother insisted that he attend college, where he followed a science curriculum in the first two years and economics in the third (because a family friend, Prasanta Chandra Mahalanobis, had assured him a job if he graduated in economics). But during this period, at the cost of his studies, he spent an increasing amount of time on his two passions: watching movies and listening to classical music. He shifted his focus from stars to directors, avidly studying the works of great film-makers such as Ernst Lubitsch, Frank Capra, John Ford and William Wyler.

After graduating from college in 1939, at the age of eighteen, Ray decided to give up further studies and focus on getting a job as a commercial artist, which he felt he could do even without formal training since he had a natural flair for drawing. His mother, however, felt he was too young to take up a regular job and suggested he study painting at the Visva-Bharati University in Santiniketan, West Bengal. The university was founded by India's great poet-mystic Rabindranath Tagore, who had been a close friend of both his grandfather and father. The desire to learn about Indian arts, to become successful as a commercial artist and to respect his mother's wishes and the lure of Tagore were too strong to ignore. After initial resistance, he agreed to enrol and spent two years at the university.

It is important to consider another influence besides that of cinema and music that created Ray the artist: Brahmo Samaj, a sect of Hinduism adopted by his family as far back as 1880 that had been formed as a reaction to orthodox Hindu practices such as sati and was influenced by Christianity and Islam. This cosmopolitan and rational outlook would later be reflected in many of Ray's films, showing a progressive outlook and a strong aversion to religious fanaticism.

At Santiniketan, during trips to nearby villages for sketching exercises, the city-bred Ray had his first encounter with rural India. In this period, he also discovered the Oriental arts: Indian sculpture and miniature painting, Japanese woodcuts and Chinese landscapes. Up until then his only exposure to art had been the works of the Western masters. He, along with three friends, undertook a long tour of places of artistic interest in the country. This was when he truly began to appreciate the nuances of Indian art. It made him see how small details could make a great impact—a quality that his films would portray; a quality that his art teacher, Binode Behari Mukherjee, also demonstrated in his own work. Thirty years later, Ray would make a loving documentary on him called *The Inner Eye*.

During these two years he pursued his two great passions, but despite his great love of cinema, the thought of becoming a film-maker had not yet occurred to him. In August 1941, Rabindranath Tagore died—a great loss to the school and to the nation. As 1942 drew to a close, Ray realized how much he missed city life. On weekends home, he would watch as many films as possible, buy records at flea markets, look for bargains on books and visit not only his mother but also his cousin Bijoya, who lived in the same family house as his mother, and with whom he was falling more and more deeply in love. In remote Santiniketan, Ray had begun to feel out of touch with what was happening in Calcutta, in India and in the world. Mahatma Gandhi had just launched the Quit India Movement against the British Empire; World War II was at Calcutta's doorstep; and he had missed Orson Welles's *Citizen Kane*, which had only played for a few days in the city. In December 1942, the Japanese bombed Calcutta for the first time and Ray left Santiniketan for good and returned home.

In April 1943, he joined the British-run advertising agency D.J. Keymer as a junior visualizer and spent the next thirteen years with the firm, where he produced many innovative advertising campaigns and created four new fonts: Ray Roman, Ray Bizarre, Daphnis and Holiday Script.

When his colleague D.K. Gupta branched out on his own with the publishing house Signet Press, he roped Ray in to illustrate books and their jackets. In 1945, Gupta published an abridged version of the novel *Pather Panchali* by Bibhuti Bhushan Banerjee, which Ray illustrated. Until then, he had not read much Bengali literature and, by his own admission, not even much of Tagore's writings. But the book made a lasting impression on him, especially after Gupta, a former film magazine editor, remarked to him that it would make a good film. His long association with Signet Press provided Ray an opportunity to read Bengali literature, and some of the books he illustrated, he would later adapt for films.

The aftermath of World War II saw Calcutta flooded with American GIs and, consequently, a sudden proliferation of Hollywood films being screened—a veritable feast for Ray and his friends. In 1947, with the help of a few friends including Bansi Chandragupta and Chidananda Dasgupta, Ray co-founded Calcutta's first film society. *Battleship Potemkin* was the first film they screened. Soon, Ray started writing and publishing articles on cinema in newspapers and magazines, both in English and Bengali. He developed another interest as well: writing screenplays for his own pleasure.

In 1949, the famous French film director Jean Renoir arrived in Calcutta to scout locations for *The River*, a film based on a book of the same name. Perhaps realizing that another opportunity of this sort would not likely come his way again, Ray walked into the hotel where Renoir was staying and sought a meeting. Soon the two were scouting for locations together in the outskirts of the city every weekend. Seeing Ray's enthusiasm and knowledge about cinema, Renoir asked him if he was planning on becoming a film-maker. To his own surprise, Ray said yes and proceeded to give him a brief outline of *Pather Panchali*, which he had recently illustrated.

Meanwhile, Ray and Bijoya had married. They were united in love, and in their mutual love of cinema and music, and would stay together in harmony all their lives.

Renoir returned to shoot his film in and around Calcutta and hired several of Ray's close friends as part of the crew. Ray was quite disappointed at not being able to participate because he had been made art director of his firm and was sent to London to work in the agency's head office. Ray and Bijoya travelled to London by ship—a journey that took sixteen days. He had carried a notebook with him on that journey in which he made notes on how he would film *Pather Panchali*: to be shot on actual locations with new faces and no make-up. His friends had reacted negatively to this idea since shooting on location with amateur actors was thought to be unfeasible in an era when all around the world films were shot on sound stages with well-known actors.

During his six months abroad, Ray saw about 100 films, including Vittorio De Sica's *The Bicycle Thief*, which made a profound impression on him. It reconfirmed his conviction that it *was* possible to make realistic cinema with an almost entirely amateur cast and shoot in actual locations. Later he would write: 'All through my stay in London, the lessons of *The Bicycle Thief* and neorealist cinema stayed with me.'

By the time he made the return journey home in late 1950, he had completed his treatment of *Pather Panchali*. With absolutely no experience in moviemaking, he collected a group of friends to work as technicians on the proposed film project. Subrata Mitra was to be the cinematographer, Anil Choudhury the production controller and Bansi Chandragupta the art director. While looking for backers, he obtained the rights to the story from the writer's widow. She gave her verbal approval and, later, much to her credit, stuck by her word despite a better financial offer. To explain the concept of his film to potential producers, Ray developed the first of his unique script books, or kheror khata as they were called, which were later to become famous. He filled a small notebook with sketches, dialogue and the treatment. This 'script', along with another sketchbook illustrating the key moments of the film, were met with curiosity by producers, and though many were impressed, none agreed to finance the film. Ray spent the next two years trying to find backers.

Having met with refusal at every turn, he eventually decided that he needed to make a short segment of the film to showcase it. He borrowed money against his insurance policy and from friends and relatives, with the intention of shooting on Sundays since he was still working at the advertising agency. In October 1952, he set out to take the first shot: the scene where Apu and his sister Durga discover the train in the field of kash flowers. The following Sunday, when they returned to resume filming, they discovered, to their horror, that the entire field of flowers had been eaten up by a herd of cattle! Ray had to wait for the next season's flowers to complete the scene and would later write: 'One day's work with camera and actors taught me more than all the dozen books I have read.'

Undaunted by obstacles, he went ahead with the job of casting and scouting locations for his film. The cast he gathered was a mix of professional actors and a few with no prior experience in acting. And then, finally, in 1953 he found a producer, Rana Dutta, who provided some funds, with a promise of more after seeing the results and post the release of his latest film. Ray took a month's leave of absence without pay and began shooting a few more sequences in Boral village. As he later recalled, this period was a great learning experience for him.

The project appeared to be shaping up well when Dutta's movie was released and turned out to be a flop, drying up all funds. Since Ray had already made arrangements for the shoot, he pawned his wife's jewellery, with her consent, and filming continued for a few days longer. A total of about 4,000 feet of film resulted from this effort, and was turned down by all the producers he showed it to.

In September 1953, Ray's son and only child was born. Sandip would grow up to share his father's passion for film and assist him in many of his masterpieces. For Ray, Sandip's birth was the only light in a dark tunnel of two years' worth of rejections.

Finally, someone suggested approaching the

Government of West Bengal and, incredibly, it agreed to fund the film. After a break of almost a year, filming resumed in the early part of 1954, but it happened in instalments since this was how government money was sanctioned, each time after endless bureaucratic protocols and paperwork. Ray later said that it was a real miracle that the two child actors did not grow up and the actress who played the old aunt did not die before the film was completed!

In the autumn of 1954, Monroe Wheeler, the director of Museum of Modern Art (MoMA), New York, was in Calcutta setting up an exhibition, and chanced upon stills from Ray's film. He was so impressed that he offered to hold a world premiere for the film at the museum once it was completed. Six months later, veteran director John Huston came to India to scout locations for *The Man Who Would Be King*. Wheeler had requested Huston to check on the progress of Ray's film and Huston gave it rave reviews based on the twenty-minute silent rough-cut Ray could show him. The MoMA premiere was on!

To meet the museum deadline, Ray and his editor worked for ten days and nights continuously during the final stage of post-production. The first print of the film came out the night before it was to be dispatched. There was no time or money for subtitles. Weeks after the screening, a letter arrived from MoMA describing at length how well the film had been received by the audience.

A few months later, in August 1955, *Pather Panchali* was released in Calcutta. The film did only moderately well in the first two weeks, but by the third week word had spread and it was running to packed houses in three cinemas, then at another cinema chain for seven more weeks. It was a hit. When Jawaharlal Nehru saw the film, he was so moved that he made arrangements for it to be shown at the Cannes Film Festival as India's official entry, where it won a special prize for Best Human Document.

Pather Panchali went on to win a dozen awards at home and at festivals abroad. It was this recognition that persuaded Ray to take the plunge. He decided to give up advertising and turn to film-making full time; and thus began a long and illustrious career. The success of his first film gave Ray full creative control over his subsequent films as writer, director, casting director, editor and composer. He went on to make a feature film every year, plus several documentaries, for the next thirty-six years.

When I met him, he already had twenty-six memorable films to his credit as well as worldwide acclaim. Looking back at that time, I am amazed that I had the nerve to approach him as a young greenhorn with just one movie to my name. But perhaps it reminded him of his own daring in approaching the great Renoir. I can only thank my stars and his kindness for the opportunity he gave me to learn, to grow, to become better, to have an understanding of film-making that I never would have had without his example and the lessons he taught me.

3

Shatranj Ke Khilari: The Beginnings

♟♟♟♞♟♟

My second encounter with Satyajit Ray and acquaintance with a whole new side of him came in the form of a surprise: the prolific amount of correspondence he generated in spite of his incredibly busy schedule. No sooner had we agreed to work together than his letters began arriving; letters which, as it turns out, document the history of how *Shatranj Ke Khilari* was made. Reviewing this correspondence and the extensive photographs I had collected, and realizing their intrinsic value, planted the seed of the idea of this book. I had been blessed with the opportunity of working closely with this great man on a highly acclaimed film and was in possession of invaluable information and an insight into how he worked. And this coupled with my own experience of all aspects of the film's creation. It was as if

I were almost duty-bound to create an engaging account of the making of this film and share it with the world.

The film we agreed to make was based on a well-known, long short story by Munshi Premchand (1880–1936) called 'Shatranj Ke Khilari'. Premchand is recognized as the foremost writer of Hindi and Urdu literature of the early twentieth century, perhaps because he was the first to write on the pertinent issues of the day, instead of escapist fantasies of kings and queens which had dominated Hindi literature up to that point. His body of work includes several novels, over 300 short stories, plays, essays and letters.

The story begins with a one-line explanation that it was the era of the reign of Nawab Wajid Ali Shah in Lucknow and then proceeds to tell the tale of two local noblemen addicted to playing chess, even to the detriment of their marital lives. Ray must have read the story set in a north Indian milieu and filed it away in his mind as a potential project beyond his familiar Bengali context. When I approached him to make a Hindi film something clicked. He took this simple story, and in due course, wove it into a complex dual-plot screenplay that involved the politics of that era and two chess players.

The screenplay Ray ultimately created is set in 1856, on the eve of the revolt of 1857, in the north Indian kingdom of Awadh (also known as Oudh), whose capital is Lucknow. It depicts the life and times of the divided—and at times deluded—Indian monarchs of the era as the East India Company went about usurping their power and wealth. There are two narratives in the story: one focuses on the confrontation between the bullish and pragmatic British general James Outram and the diffident response of the cultured, artistically talented but head-in-the-clouds Muslim king of Awadh, Wajid Ali Shah, whose throne is in the process of being appropriated by the British. The second is the tragicomic tale of two rich noblemen of this kingdom, inseparable friends obsessed with the game of chess to the point of neglecting their responsibilities and their wives, oblivious of the momentous tide of history about to sweep over them. The game of chess becomes a metaphor not only for the power struggle between the Indian king and the British Empire but also for the domestic struggles of the chess players and the machinations of their neglected wives.

~

As he had indicated during our first meeting, Ray intended to write the script himself, like he always did for his films. It was now only a matter of fulfilling prior obligations so he could start working on *Shatranj Ke Khilari*. In the interim, letters went back and forth between us. These letters trace the trajectory of the film's development and offer a peek into Ray's mind and style of working. They piece together the inside story of the making of *The Chess Players*.

26/3/75

Dear Suresh,

I don't know if you are permanently residing at the Shalimar Hotel and whether this will reach you. I hope it does. I am deeply immersed in the shooting of the new film[1] and bracing myself for a hectic spell of Calcutta street outdoors starting 1 April.

The present film will keep me busy till July. After that there's a Moscow trip (ten days). Around mid-August I should be [able], with limitation, to start on the screenplay of *The Chess Players*. I should warn you that the adaptation is not going to be an easy job. However, I have already done all the reading up on the background and that should help.

I reckon we should be able to start shooting by December.

Give me a ring if and when you are in Calcutta next.

Best,

Satyajit Ray

---

1. *Jana Aranya* (*The Middle Man*).

25/6/75

Dear Suresh,

I really don't know how to thank you for the magnificent birthday gift. A really splendid book:[2] it was most thoughtful of you to have sent it. We should have finished our shooting by now, but a fresh spate of load shedding[3] coupled with bad weather has upset our schedule a bit, so that we still have 5/6 days' shooting left. This should be over in the next ten/twelve days.

My mind is now slowly but surely turning to *The Chess Players*. I have just cancelled a week's invitation to Moscow (10–16 July) and could come down instead to Bombay for a couple of days, if only to talk to Sanjeev[4] and discuss other casting possibilities—if you feel delay could create problems. By the way, I want Asrani for the role of Wajid Ali Shah; and could you find out about the possibility of getting Saeed Jaffrey to play the other main character. You can write to BBC London for his address. But on second thoughts—wait till I get to Bombay. I believe the word has already spread in Bombay, in which case my visit must be kept totally hush-hush.

My original plan was to come to Bombay after finishing the rough cut at the end of July. I'll wait for your advice on this. I'll start work on the screenplay in the beginning of August, and will in any case be at Rajkamal[5] at the end

---

2. *The Poster in History* by Max Gallo.

3. Power outages in a locality.

4. Sanjeev Kumar, the actor Ray wanted to cast for the role of Mirza, one of the chess players.

5. Rajkamal Studios, Bombay.

of August for my RR[6]—by which time the rough outline of the screenplay should have taken shape. Even on the basis of the ideas forming in my head, I can say that the background alone to *The Chess Players* will make it a fairly big and expensive film. I hope this doesn't dismay you. As for the dialogue, I'll write in English, and will need someone to translate and, if necessary, to elaborate—in conjunction with me. If the Bengali-knowing Urdu writer is really good, then I could write in Bengali. Of course, I'll try to get a working knowledge of Urdu before I actually start shooting.

I have a fortnight's trip to UK and USA in October, but before that—sometime in September—a week's trip to Lucknow will be necessary. Bansi[7] must try and be free to come with me. All paperwork on the film should be over by November in order to start shooting in January and February. This should be adequate for all outdoors and some of the indoors. I must be free in March to prepare my Norton lectures[8] in Harvard for April and May. This is a great honour, but also a great nuisance in view of *The Chess Players*, which I would have loved to shoot without interruption. Harvard will keep me chained through April–May, so that shooting could only be resumed in June. I reckon approximately sixty days' shooting. More when

6. Re-recording: the combining of many soundtracks in the final mix.

7. Bansi Chandragupta, one of the finest art directors in Indian cinema.

8. A prominent lecture series at Harvard which Ray was asked to deliver that year.

we meet—but let me know if you want me in Bombay in mid-July or later.

Best,

Yours,

Manik-da

P.S. A remarkable piece of luck plus coincidence—a Bengali translation of a definite nineteenth-century Urdu work on the Nawabi period in Lucknow called *Guzeshta Lucknow* has just been put out by Sahitya Akademi. A fantastic work—literally an encyclopaedia.

Dear Suresh,

Bansi wrote to say Sanjeev will be away in Bangalore for some days, and will be back in Bombay in the first week of August. The time that suits me best for a flying visit is not too long after 4/5 August. I would definitely prefer to see Sanjeev in Bombay rather than elsewhere. Let us say between the 5 and 10. You have to make sure that Sanjeev will be in town. Try and give me at least three days' notice. Best is to phone before 9 a.m. in the morning or latish in the evening.

In a hurry,

Manik-da

~

It was very gratifying to know that Ray was now starting to write the script for our film and also immersing himself in the casting. I had been told that he wrote his original version of scripts in traditional clothbound notebooks called khatas, and that they were more like a research scientist's lab notes than ordinary scripts. Being both an artist and a musician, Ray was very visual, and his khatas reflected this. In them he would draw the frames of the shots on the left-hand side and write the dialogues on the right. They would also contain references to his research materials as well as notes on music and sound effects.

Fascinated by the exceptional script book he had created for our film, I once asked him if I might have it, thinking that as producer perhaps it was appropriate for me to keep it. 'No, I'm sorry, Suresh, but all my khatas are carefully preserved by the French Cinémathèque in their film archives,' was his reply. The script book of *Pather Panchali*, his first film and one of the great classics of all time, had also been sent to the Cinémathèque. Years later, when he wanted them to loan it to someone researching his work it was found to be missing, and this was devastating for him. It was subsequently recovered and recently published as a book by my publishers, HarperCollins.

Our actual working script was typed by Ray himself and even the corrections were made in his own handwriting. He sent me the original and kept a copy for himself, which I thought was a rare gesture on his part.

When he handed me the English version of the script, he told me that he openly welcomed any sort of advice and discussion regarding the story and the choice of cast, and later selected a few actors based on my suggestions. We also had a short discussion about the working conditions he expected, such as authority over the final cut, payments and modes of payment, casting (mutually agreed between the two of us) and various other points.

The project seemed to be well on its way by late summer of 1975, with shooting tentatively moved from December 1975 to January or February of the coming year, when a medical problem felled me.

4 September 1975
Shri Satyajit Ray,
Calcutta

Dear Shri Satyajit Ray,

I am writing this on behalf of Shri Suresh Jindal, who, as you may be aware, was hospitalized for some time. He has asked me to inform you that he was operated upon for an abscess in his hip and will have to be confined to bed for a few more days. As soon as he is fit to move about, he will get in touch with you by phone. He is planning to visit Calcutta by the 15 of this month, provided his doctors permit him to do so.

With regards,
Yours sincerely,
for Suresh Jindal,
KHM Subramanian

CC
Shri Bansi Chandragupta
Bombay—for information please

~

I had managed to get a liver abscess—a serious condition requiring immediate hospitalization. The doctor explained that it was quite common for students of boarding schools to contract this disease from contaminated food. His diagnosis was a huge relief, because I had begun to think that I might have destroyed my liver due to excessive drinking. Contaminated food made sense. Besides my boarding school days, I did not have a place of my own in Bombay. I had left my home in New Delhi for long periods of hectic activity in Bombay during my first film, when I usually stayed at the cheapest guesthouses or hotels (of the hire-by-hour sort for clandestine rendezvous) to utilize all available funds for my film. And my drinking was legendary.

I was part of the gang of 'new cinema' makers—all of us potential Rays, Godards, Fellinis and Kurosawas who were going to turn mainstream Indian 'formula' cinema on its head. We were ambitious, enthusiastic, hardworking and all hard drinkers. We exemplified the old joke in the film industry:

Question: 'Why do you drink so much?'
Answer: 'Because my film is a hit.'
Question: 'Why do you drink so much?'
Answer: 'Because my film is a flop.'

After slogging all day in editing rooms, studios, locations and cheap hotel rooms (where we had our brainstorming 'story and script' meetings), we headed out to the suburbs to our favourite 'aunty's adda' for the best part of our labours: extended drinking sessions. In those days, Bombay was not the massive megalopolis it is today. The suburbs were still suburbs in the true sense, with bungalows and two- or three-storey houses with lawns and gardens. High-rises had only begun to sprout then. Juhu, which is now crawling with hotels, had only three at the time; and beyond that were the boondocks. Those were also the days of prohibition, but just like in the Roaring Twenties in the US, booze was available everywhere. 'Aunty's adda' was a euphemism for a speakeasy. These addas were located in slums, dockyards, in buildings under construction and in the fishing villages and beach shacks on the Arabian Sea. They were called such because women ran them while their menfolk sat drinking with us, or huddled in backrooms making deals.

If you ran out of booze at a late-night party, all you had to do was summon the lift operator of your apartment building and he invariably just 'happened to know someone' in the nearby slums, or the next building, who 'happened' to have a ready stock of whatever you needed. All taxi drivers were familiar with the buildings in the suburbs where, from the second or third floor, an empty basket was first lowered to receive your money, pulled up and lowered again, with a bottle in it this time.

Bombay was a more innocent and simpler city in those days. 'Organized crime' consisted of bootlegging and smuggling; and a form of gambling called matka was run by kingpin Rattan Khatri. Everyone played matka, a numbers game akin to lotto, in the hope of making a quick fortune. Slum dwellers played for as low as Re. 1 and the industrialists of Malabar and Cumballa Hills staked thousands of dollars. The city's Godfather-type don was Haji Mastan, whose rags-to-riches life was portrayed by Salim–Javed in the blockbuster *Deewaar* starring Amitabh Bachchan. Soft drugs such as hashish, marijuana and opium were sold in 'licensed' shops, and these were mostly located in the alleys and slums near temples and other places of worship. There were no hard drugs available on the streets since only the rich could afford cocaine and psychedelics.

After you and your friend got dead drunk at the adda, 'aunty' would call a cab and sternly tell the driver to take each of you to your respective doorsteps and to ring the doorbell to ensure that someone would take charge. The cabbie either collected the fare from the folks at home or was prepaid. Not once in all those years was there a report of an incident of anyone getting mugged or cheated, or not being delivered home safely. It was an 'honourable' mafia which did not harm innocents, nor allowed them to be harmed by petty crooks and criminals, for in their eyes (and in ours) they were not criminals but providers of a service that all of us indulged in.

Every residential building, every studio, every office had its 'door-to-door smuggling-wala' (like a travelling salesman) who came neatly dressed, was infinitely polite and patient, and carried a briefcase full of contraband that you had previously ordered, such as eau de cologne, perfume, razors and blades, blank audio cassettes, and catalogues listing the items you might want to order in future, such as watches, music systems, cameras and just about everything you could possibly need or desire. Nobody was committing a crime: It was just dhandha—a marvellously rich Hindi word meaning 'business' or 'slogging to keep the home fires burning'. All the politicos, bureaucrats and cops got their regular hafta—their weekly bribe. Under our Soviet-style socialism, the nation was perpetually broke, with an average growth rate of 2–3 per cent per annum. The official sanctioned amount of foreign exchange for travel abroad was $200 a day for business travel and a total of $11 for a tourist trip, and a ton of documentation to change a film-related trip or a pleasure trip to business travel. Of course, this system made criminals of all who went abroad, because to get the much-needed extra dollars we had to arrange for it through the black market via our ever-obliging smuggling-wala.

In the end, *everybody* was a winner in this system. The Bombay Police of the time had a reputation of being the most efficient sleuths because they used the underworld as their eyes and ears to spot 'illegal' dhandha-walas, and thus no outside thugs had a chance of surviving in the city. When a rare rape or murder of 'innocents' did occur between the mafiosi during turf wars, it had all of us—the imbibers and consumers, the aunties and door-to-door smuggling-walas—in conniptions, ranting against the monster for giving the dhandha-walas a bad name. Under their honour code with the police, it was the mafia's duty to find the offenders and either eliminate them or bring them to book. And they always delivered. Even the cunning master escapist Charles Sobhraj, who had hoodwinked the finest police forces in the world, was finally nabbed by Bombay Police.

~

My illness lasted a long time, because the standard cure for a liver abscess was a strong injection of antibiotic in the hip upon arrival at the hospital, and this sometimes caused an abscess in the area, which it did in my case.

Thus, I had to go in for surgery and the abscess had to be drained constantly, resulting in my having to stay more than two weeks in the hospital and another six to eight weeks recuperating.

In the early part of my illness, I did not mind being comatose as much as I minded not being able to visit my 'aunty' or place an order with my smuggling-wala. But after a while, I was terribly impatient to get out of the hospital, as we urgently needed supplies for the forthcoming film. And Hamid bhai, my very own smuggling-wala, was a wizard at catering to my needs, and during hard times, most generous in extending credit.

'Brother Suresh, you are from a good family. I know you will honour your debts,' Hamid said. When one day I asked him teasingly, 'Hamid bhai, what will you do if I run back home to Delhi?' his laconic reply was, 'Then Allah is bountiful. Please tell me what you want.'

Calcutta
18 Sept. 75

Dear Suresh,

It wasn't possible to discuss the film over the phone the other day: there were at least six other people in the room.

As I told you in Bombay, Sanjeev is no problem. Our major problem seems to be money. I see no possibility of the budget being kept below 30/35 lakhs. It is true that about 70 per cent of the film will have nothing to do with what one normally associates with a historical film, but for the rest we shall need all the trappings.

Problem two: what with my US tour in Oct. and all the preliminary paperwork etc., the soonest we can start shooting is in February '76. In April I have to go to Harvard for six weeks for the Norton lectures. This will mean holding up production for at least three months— including March when I have to prepare the lectures. Apart from being uneconomical, this will mean resuming shooting at the height of summer. I have done this kind of thing many times in the last twenty years, but am extremely reluctant to do so on my first Hindi film.

All in all I feel it would be wisest to plan for Oct '76, shooting right through winter. With a whole year to go, we can even think of less expensive subjects—in case money remains a problem with you, and in case the story should prove to be intractable.

I hope to see you in Bombay. Meanwhile, give the matter some thought.

I hope you are 100 per cent fit by now.

All the best,

Manik-da

Bombay
27 September 1975

Dear Manik-da,

Thank you very much for your letter. As I discussed with you over the phone, I was planning to come to

Bombay while you are still there. But unfortunately my injected abscess developed further complications about a week ago, for which, along with the daily dressing and cleaning of the wound, I now have to go to the hospital for electric treatment.

As regards the postponement of *The Chess Players* to October next year, I also feel that in view of the problems mentioned by you it may be advisable. Added to that, of course, is my physical incapability as well as your intended trip to the USA in the coming month.

The doctors feel that it may take another two weeks for the abscess to heal to the point where it does not require daily dressing. I still hope that I may be able to meet you in Calcutta before you leave for America so that we could discuss the details further.

I hope the re-recording of your film is going smoothly and I pray for its success.

Thanking you,

Yours sincerely,

Suresh

~

The rest of 1975 wore on without much work on the film. I spent the months recovering while Manik-da continued with his prior obligations. It was discouraging to be faced with a whole year's wait before we could shoot our film, but it was obvious the gods intended it that way, and there was nothing to do but accept it.

4

Research and Scheduling

♟♟♟♛♟♟

The year 1976 arrived. Having recovered from the abscess, I turned all my attention to *Shatranj Ke Khilari*, laying the groundwork for contacts, locations, casting, etc.— the many small details that go into the preparation of a film. I was becoming increasingly excited as we approached the start of filming when catastrophe struck: Sanjeev Kumar, one of our lead actors who was to play the nobleman Mirza, suffered a major heart attack. Fortunately, he survived, but he needed over four months to recover. And no sooner had he been well than Amjad Khan, set to play the nawab of Awadh, Wajid Ali Shah, had a near-fatal car crash. His chest was crushed and he almost died. It took him over three to four months to recover.

Though I felt terrible for both men, I couldn't help but

feel sorry for myself as well, wondering if our production was jinxed and if I would ever be able to bring this project to fruition. Right through the making of the film, I couldn't shrug off the fear of things falling through and my dream of making a film with Ray not being realized. I guess it is human nature to fear the worst when you wish for something with all your heart. Setting such negative thoughts aside, I continued to do my bit every day, trying to procure what was needed and completing the tasks that I was responsible for. Meanwhile, the many correspondences on various aspects of the film continued.

Shri Suresh Jindal,
Lucknow
16 February 1976

Dear Shri Jindal,

I acknowledge the receipt of your letter dated the 12. I was in Delhi since the 9 of this month and have returned only this morning, so I could not reply to your letter earlier. You are most welcome at my place along with Shri Satyajit Ray and Shri Rajendra Yadav.[1] I shall be happy to serve

---

1. A Hindi writer who put us in touch with Amritlal Nagar. His wife, Mannu Bhandari, also a writer, wrote the story on which my film *Rajnigandha* was based.

you with whatever little knowledge I have of my home town.

Best regards,
Yours sincerely,
Amritlal Nagar[2]

12 February 1976

My dear Manik-da,

Namaskar. As discussed with you over the phone, I hope we can go to Lucknow on Monday, 23 February. I have already got in touch with some people I know there who will be able to help and guide us during our stay there. Please confirm if this date is suitable for you. Also do let me know the status of your trip to the USA.

I hope by the time I meet you we will be able to finalize the cast of the film. In this connection, I would like to make a suggestion that we take a known star as one of our leading ladies. I do not know how you feel about it, but would it be possible for us to cast Raakhee? I venture to make this suggestion since selecting her will not affect the artistic integrity of the film, and yet would also make it commercially more viable in view of our large budget.

Also, I understand you were very impressed by the performance of Amjad Khan in *Sholay*. Will it be possible to cast him in the role of Wajid Ali Shah?

The minor operation I had undergone was for a fissure

---

2. A famous writer based in Lucknow.

which had been bothering me for a long time, and now that it is over, I will be absolutely healthy to devote all my time to our upcoming project.

My best regards to you and your family.

Yours sincerely,

Suresh

Calcutta
16 February 1976

Dear Suresh,

Many thanks for your letter. I'm delighted to know you are up and about again. I'm afraid Lucknow is impossible for the 23. I'm just about to start a short film on Balasaraswati[3] (I may have told you about it). We go to Madras on the 26 and shoot from 1 to 15 March. A good date for Lucknow would be 20 March. This is no problem since the Harvard trip has been postponed by a year. Let me know if 20 suits you.

As I told you, things will really get going on *The Chess Players* from June. I understand your impatience but I see no cause for alarm. Five months is ample time for any preparations we may want to do for the film. So don't start worrying about the cast yet. I can assure you that I'm not going to use unknowns in the two female parts ... Amjad is a good tip for Wajid, but I can only decide after a personal

---

3. Documentary about Balasaraswati, a famous Bharatanatyam dancer.

encounter. The rest we shall discuss when we meet. By the way, I think it'll have to be the writer you suggested for the collaboration (was it Nagore?),[4] rather than Kaifi.[5] Kaifi doesn't know a word of English, let alone Bengali.

All the best.

Yours,

Manik-da

18 February 1976

My dear Manik-da,

Thank you for your kind letter dated 16 February 1976, which I just received. I am out of hospital and am perfectly fit. The date 20 March 1976 suggested by you for our visit to Lucknow will be suitable for me.

I have noted what you have to say on the other points.

With best regards,

Yours sincerely,

Suresh

---

4. Amritlal Nagar.

5. Kaifi Azmi, well-known Urdu writer and poet, and also the father of Shabana Azmi, the actress who played the wife of Mirza in the film.

19 February 1976

My dear Manik-da,

I had got in touch with Mr Amritlal Nagar and enclose herein a copy of his letter to me. I have informed him regarding the postponement of our trip. If you so wish I can sound him out on the possibility that we would like the dialogues of *The Chess Players* to be written by him. So far I have not mentioned this matter. I have only asked him to help us with the general research.

Could you please send me the reference of the English translation of *Guzeshta Lucknow*, as my brother is leaving for England on Sunday, 22 February 1976? I shall ask him to send a copy.

My best wishes for your success of *Jana Aranya*.

Yours sincerely,

Suresh

21/2/76

Dear Suresh,

Thanks for your letter. You don't have to tell Nagar just now that he'll write the dialogue. Let him give expert advice at this stage. If I find him good and easy to work with then he could be assigned to translate my dialogues and add embellishments if necessary.

Here are the details on the English version of *Guzeshta Lucknow*:

Lucknow: The Last Phase of an Oriental Culture by
Abdul Halim Sharar (translated and edited by E.S.
Harcourt and Fakhir Hussain) (published by Elek at
£12.50)

Jana Aranya opened yesterday. Reports so far are very
good. Sorry for the rush.

Yours,

Manik-da

~

As I was beginning to find out, Ray was a tireless and
outstanding researcher. His capacity and love for it
was prodigious. His mind was like a steel trap, focused
only on the subject at hand. Every available space in his
study was now piled high with books on chess, James
Outram's Blue Books from the National Library, books
and reproductions of Company School paintings, the
Daniells and other master printmakers and painters
of Indian landscapes and architecture, miscellaneous
travelogues and every other possible kind of information
on the ambience, food, clothing, mannerisms, music, etc.
of the period in which the story was set. When it came to
research and learning anything new, he had the curiosity
and inquisitiveness of a child.

I observed him immerse himself in the preparation
of the film. Just accompanying him to meetings with
scholars, academicians, experts and specialists in music,
art, architecture and military history was an amazing

experience and taught me a great deal. We also went to museums, the havelis of aristocratic Lucknawis and the thakur baris of north Calcutta. From the Imperial War Museum and the India Office Library to the Falaknuma Palace of the nizams of Hyderabad and the City Palace Museum in Jaipur—it was like researching the period for a PhD. One evening we would be having dinner with the Rajmata of Jaipur and the next morning searching for an expert on the Shia namaz in the winding alleys of old Lucknow. It was like a magical mystery tour: psychedelic all the way, in every way.

And what was always most evident was the utmost respect he bestowed on anyone who helped widen his knowledge. His impeccable reputation opened many doors for us, but he was always genuinely grateful that people were so kind, perhaps because he didn't fully grasp his own greatness and fame.

Delhi
4 March 1976

My dear Manik-da,

I hope the shooting of the documentary has been completed and everything is going on smoothly. I am leaving for Bombay tomorrow and will be back in Delhi by the 10. In case there is some matter on which you want to contact me before I return, my address in Bombay is as follows:

Suresh Jindal
C/o Taj Mahal Hotel
Bombay - 400 001
Yours sincerely,
Suresh

4/3/76

Dear Suresh,

I'm here in Madras working on the documentary on Balasaraswati. We expect to be back in Calcutta around the 16 or so. I shall certainly be in a position to make the Lucknow trip on the 20. I hope you will make necessary arrangements in the meantime. Must thing for you would be to give me a call on the 18 or so, and let me know if everything's OK.

I hope this finds you well.

Yours,
Manik-da

~

Everywhere we went people were awed by Ray's talent and fame. When we finally managed to coordinate our schedules and reach Amritlal Nagar's house in Lucknow, the aged writer welcomed us with delight and these words: 'This is the happiest day for this small house of

mine. I feel deeply respected and obliged by your visit.'
As always, Manik-da shied away from the praise, never
quite able to decide what to do on these occasions.

Nagar-ji showed us around his haveli where it is
believed Wajid Ali Shah spent his last evening. He also
showed us his research room, which resembled an
intellectual's den from the Middle Ages. Of particular
interest was a raised platform covered by a green sheet
on which sat his low Indian-style desk where he had
composed and written many great novels. During the
visit, Ray and Nagar discussed Premchand and *Shatranj
Ke Khilari*, Wajid Ali Shah, the costumes and fashion
of the period, as well as the manner of life and social
relationships in nineteenth-century Lucknow. Nagar-ji
showed us his paintings, prints, photos and an original
brick from Ayodhya's famed Laxman ka Teela. He
bowed his head and prayed in front of photographs of
Premchand and Saratchandra Chatterjee, telling us that
they were his gurus.

Since Ray and Nagar were both experts in Bengali,
they immediately formed a close bond, and I could see
Manik-da's delight at such a rare exchange of ideas. As we
left, he remarked: 'Suresh, every film is like an adventure!'
In fact, for him it was more: It was a secret journey into his
own creative world. His quest was not only for knowledge
but also for wisdom and personal growth.

Long after our visit, the two men kept up a friendly

correspondence. In later years, whenever I visited Lucknow and stopped off at Nagar-ji's, the first thing he would ask about was Manik-da's well-being and activities.

12 April 1976
New Delhi

My dear Manik-da,

I have written to Pustak Kendra, Lucknow, to send you a set of the Rare India series. I have also sent them the payment, so please do not pay if they inadvertently send you a bill.

As the starting time for *The Chess Players* is getting closer, I would like to make you privy to a few thoughts:

1. I am hoping that by now a more complete budget can be set down. Maybe your production manager Mr Anil Choudhury can start on it. Since a lot of our shooting is to be done in the studios, an idea of the set costs is important. In this matter I have no experience, as *Rajnigandha* had no sets. In this case, we have to allow for some extravagance on Bansi-da's part. Everyone agrees he is a fine set designer (perhaps the best we have) but everyone also agrees on his extravagance.

2. Regarding casting: a rough sale price would work out as follows:

If negative cost is 35 lakhs[6]

6. Until now Ray's most expensive film had cost 10 lakh rupees. My first film cost 7 lakh rupees.

Cost of quota prints and levy would be 10 lakhs

Total: 45 lakhs

The cost of each territory (there are six, including overseas) comes to 7.5 lakhs at break even. To that has to be added 20 per cent for interest payments, production publicity, unforeseen contingencies and producer's profit. This is a rough rule of thumb. Therefore, the sales cost comes to about 9 lakhs.

For a film of this kind, the territories of CPCI (i.e., Madhya Pradesh, Rajasthan and parts of Maharashtra) and Punjab (comprising of Punjab, Haryana, Himachal and Jammu & Kashmir) may be hard to sell initially. Even later, they may have to be given at a lower price. This necessitates asking a higher price for the other circuits, say 10 lakhs.

An asking price of 10 lakhs requires some padding in the casting. Sanjeev and Saeed have been finalized as the chess players. I hope Amjad Khan can be fixed for Wajid Ali's role, since apart from being an actor of promise, he is also becoming more 'saleable'. That leaves us some leeway only in the female casting. Even though the female roles are not very long in the film, for the distributors a big name on the marquee has an initial draw.

In Lucknow we had discussed the possibility of using Hema Malini. You had felt that perhaps the role may not be attractive to her as it is small. If you feel that in other ways she can fit the bill, I am sure she will be willing. Unless you feel she may be totally incongruous in the role, I request we give her a try.

I know it will be ideal if we could get Muslim girls to do the roles, but unfortunately, the choice is very restricted. The Muslim girls we have are Zeenat Aman and Shabana Azmi. Another person who could be considered is Vidya Sinha.[7]

3. Regarding the laboratory: in Bombay films a lot of laboratory credit is given, which, as you can well appreciate, is a great relief on the resources available for production. Famous Cine Laboratories and Studios, Mahalaxmi, had given me a 50 per cent credit for *Rajnigandha* because I was a new producer using all newcomers. The owner, Shri Roongta, has been after me for this project, and I can get very advantageous terms. Besides that they have excellent editing facilities with four brand new Steinbecks. Also, my working relation with them is excellent and they gave me very fair treatment in my rough times. I do not know what terms Gemini[8] will be willing to give us. From what I hear, they give very little or no credit. All the same, on hearing from you, I will write to them to see what they can do. Further, a lab in Bombay will also be easier logistically speaking.

4. A schedule of the outlay of funds: this could be easily worked out along with the budget. Pre-shooting expenses will mainly be on the signing amounts, preparation of costumes, general research and development. According to my calculations, our expenditures will start by June.

---

7. Her first film, *Rajnigandha*, was also my first.

8. Laboratory in Chennai where Ray processed all his films.

I write this in complete trust and frankness so as to arrive at a closer working relationship. I do hope it does not intrude upon the work at hand.

My best regards,

Yours sincerely,

Suresh

Calcutta
18 April '76

Dear Suresh,

Many thanks for your letter. The books arrived safely. A most useful bunch, and a most generous gift for which I am truly grateful. I hope you won't make a habit of this kind of generosity; it's a trait that a film producer must learn to do without!

Your letter presents the financial aspects of the production very clearly. Although I hadn't worked out the details myself, I had a hunch that this is what it would look like on paper. It only serves to strengthen the feeling that we haven't perhaps made the ideal choice in *The Chess Players*. It must be clear to you that, being a period piece involving Wajid as well as the British, the low-budget approach was ruled out automatically. The cost would be high regardless of casting. And since it would be high, the rules of the game demand a further addition by way of stars to ensure the film's saleability. But even here there are problems.

Amjad is a very good choice for Wajid, but for all I know he may have already been typed as a villain. (What has he done since *Sholay*?) In our film there won't be a trace of villainy in his part.

Hema has the drawback of looking a south Indian from a mile away. As such she would be a slur on my reputation for meticulous casting. It's true that there are quite a number of big name stars in Bombay who wouldn't mind playing comparatively small roles for me; but what about afterwards, when the public finds out they've been had? My feeling is that this sort of thing often works against a film.

My biggest stumbling block, however, is the growing impression in my mind that the story is intractable from a script point of view, or at best can make an arty, intellectual type of film which would put off the distributors. The reason for this is that I am finding it extremely difficult to put across the idea of addiction on which the development as well as the denouement of the story hangs. There would be no problem at all if we were dealing with gambling instead of chess. The idea of addiction to an intellectual game would remain at a level of abstraction—except to chess addicts—no matter how much you tried to make it psychologically believable. And the moment you got down to the business of showing the game, silence and inaction would descend upon the screen—with what consequences you may well imagine. One would be on safer grounds if the quiet moments of the play could come between scenes of strong action. Unfortunately, the annexation itself was an anti-climax—with the nawab laying down arms and the British virtually walking in and taking over.

I want another fortnight to decide whether a way out of the impasse can be found. If not, I suggest that we abandon this particular project, disregarding the publicity it has already received. I think I told you in the beginning of my habit of announcing a project only after finishing the screenplay. I've scrapped dozens of stories after a period of initial enthusiasm just because they proved unscriptable. I had to break the rule in the present instance primarily because of Sanjeev. The time has now come to decide whether we should plunge into a 50-lakh project without the backing of total conviction that it is viable. Let me know what you think.

Best,
Manik-da

Shri Satyajit Ray,
Calcutta
6 May 1976

My dear Manik-da,

I have received your letter dated 18 April 1976 and have been pondering over it ever since. Further discussion on this can better be done by meeting personally.

I am leaving for Bombay tonight. As my own flat is still not completely ready for occupation, I will be staying with Tinnu. Kindly drop me a line care of Tinnu or Bansi-da regarding your programme for Bombay. I will be in Bombay for at least three weeks.

My best regards to you and your family.

Yours sincerely,

Suresh

~

I was not privy to how Manik-da resolved the problem he mentions in the previous letter. I know he did not want to disappoint me since he was acutely aware that I had my heart and soul invested in the project. But then, he too must have had a lot at stake—his first film in Hindi. He must have wanted to do it or he would have gone in another direction. I only know I was ever so grateful when he let me know that he had solved the problem and we could move forward.

~

With the exception of boarding school and my studies abroad, I had spent most of my life in New Delhi where my family was based. With the money from my first film, I purchased a flat in Bombay, since I needed to be where the film industry is located. At the start of our film project, I had still not shifted into it but would soon do so. It goes without saying that when we were on location, we stayed in hotels that I, as the producer, provided.

As for filming locations, it was decided that all indoor scenes were to be shot at Indrapuri Studio in Calcutta, since it was the most familiar and easy option for Ray and also cheaper than any Bombay studio. For outdoor scenes, besides the city landscapes, we found a village near Lucknow; and since the horses needed for the long defile of the British troops at the end of the film could only be recruited from the 61st Cavalry Regiment of the army based in Jaipur, we ended up filming there as well. We also did a bit of patchwork filming in Bombay for a scene that had to be redone because an actor's scarf did not match the previous shots. Manik-da and I had recced all these places together during his research trips.

Wherever we went, he always worked with utmost dedication. An example of this was once when we had returned to the cool sanctuary of the hotel after scouting locations on dusty Indian plains in the blazing May sun. We had just finished lunch and all I wanted was a well-deserved siesta. Suddenly we received a call from a benefactor of Ray's saying he had some period costumes and jewellery to show us, which he also offered on loan for the filming.

'Dada, maybe you should rest awhile. May I call them back and say we'll come in the evening?' I asked, with fake oversolicitousness.

'We can go now, Baba. Just give me a few minutes to freshen up,' he responded with a smile at my not-too-well-concealed groan.

No rest for the weary around this cinema addict, I sighed to myself, but learnt an important lesson: best to pursue leads immediately, before people change their minds.

5

Casting

♟♟♟♟♟♟

No actor would have turned down an offer to work with Ray. In the early phase of his career, due to the meagre budgets available for his films, he often cast non-professionals. Tinnu Anand once told me how he had acted out the dialogue for the female lead to mimic in every shot in one of his films, who then went on to win a National Award for Best Actress!

Ray's instinct for honing an actor's performance was unerring. He appreciated even the smallest of roles played well. I remember once, after a screening of a newly released Hollywood film, *Network*, he turned to me and said: 'That's a marvellous actress. Outstanding.'

'Yes sir, Faye Dunaway was really good,' I replied, stating the obvious.

'No, no. That's not who I meant. The actress who

played the wife of William Holden. She was outstanding. Very good work.'

That year, Beatrice Straight, the British stage actress he had pointed out—unknown in Hollywood—went on to surprise the film world by winning an Oscar for Best Supporting Actress, along with Faye Dunaway's much-expected win for Best Actress. Straight was on screen for just five minutes and forty seconds—the shortest performance ever to win an Academy Award for acting. I realized then that it took a keen perception like Ray's to zero in on a brilliantly acted, but much smaller, role, especially in the presence of a more famous and accomplished actress.

When I asked him, 'Manik-da, how do you cast? I mean, what are the most important things you look for in an actor?' his instant reply was, 'The eyes, Suresh ... and the walk. These are what tell us most about ourselves.'

Like almost everyone else, actors adored him. Any advice he gave on acting, or how to do anything at all, was always spot on. When I told Shabana Azmi, a gifted actress with several memorable films to her credit, that her role in *Shatranj Ke Khilari* would be limited to two or three scenes, she replied: 'Suresh, if Ray wants me to hold a jhadu for one shot only, I will gladly do it. Work with Ray? Wow!'

In turn, Ray's respect for actors and their time was equally well known. When filming was postponed for eight months because of Sanjeev Kumar's heart attack and Amjad Khan's near-fatal accident, he wrote actor Barry John a three-page letter, explaining and apologizing for the postponement. Barry had only one scene in the film! Barry was so touched by this courtesy he never tired of mentioning it to his friends for years.[1]

~

By the summer of 1976 we were making headway both in the screenplay and in the casting. Manik-da and I shared equal responsibility in the casting process, although, as with everything on his films, he had the final say. As I recall, the only actor he was keen to cast from the start was Saeed Jaffrey. After reading the original story, it was Saeed whom he had envisioned for the role of Meer Roshan Ali, one of the chess-playing noblemen. Of course, we were aware of Indian cinema's acting pool, and, as is done everywhere, we too went in for typecasting. We were familiar with Sanjeev Kumar's work and looks, and he seemed right for Mirza Sajjad Ali, the other nobleman.

Amjad Khan, who generally played the villain after his star-making turn in *Sholay*, was my suggestion for the role of Nawab Wajid Ali Shah since he was a major box-office draw and because he was a Muslim himself. If one looks at Wajid Ali Shah's portrait, one can see an uncanny

1. Considered to be the 'father of English theatre in Delhi', Barry John played Fayrer, the resident surgeon, in the film.

resemblance between the two. Ray had his reservations about Amjad being able to rid himself of his typecasting as a villain and play a gentle soul, but Khan rendered an excellent portrayal. As for the prime minister to the nawab (Ali Naqi), acclaimed Calcutta theatre actor Victor Banerjee was Ray's choice, probably because he looked almost exactly like the prime minister, whose portrait hangs in the Hussainabad Picture Gallery Museum in Lucknow. Banerjee, whose first film role this would be, delivered a sensitive performance. He would later become famous internationally as the lead actor in David Lean's acclaimed film *A Passage to India*.

Even though Ray had serious doubts about casting the young and beautiful Shabana Azmi to play Mirza's wife who is spurned for chess, in the end she did get the role.

In time, all the roles were filled and we both felt we had selected a superb cast. When there was an eight-month-long delay in filming, it was a bit difficult to rearrange everyone's schedule, but since everyone was keen to work on a Ray film, they accommodated him first and fulfilled their other obligations later.

19 June 1976

Dear Manik-da,

I hope this finds your back ailment under control.

I am in Bombay for the time being and will be going to Delhi for a week to ten days. I will finalize my programme on hearing of your Bombay plans.

Now that the script problems are within sight of a solution, the next worry is to procure the dates of the artists. If your mind is made up with respect to Shabana and Amjad, it will be a good idea to inform them, as both are busy with a number of assignments. Particularly in the case of Shabana, as not only does she have a number of films but she has given continuous dates for most of them. On hearing from you, I will do the needful.

Also, since a lot of equipment has gone underground,[2] we will need to book it as early as possible. Sufficient time will also be needed to get the raw stock permits, etc., especially in the case of Eastman negative, as this stock has a talent of disappearing as soon as the consignment arrives in the market. I do not envisage the same problems in our case, but I would feel easier being prepared in advance.

As regards the role of Mirza's wife, I feel of all the women available, Vidya Sinha will be the best bet. She may not be very good in her histrionic talents, but she will be able to deliver under your skilled direction.

---

2. Smuggled equipment was being checked by the government, hence much of it had become unavailable.

I have received my copy of Sharar's book[3] and am going through it. Just finished *The Peacock Throne*. Marvellous reading: and as you observed, Dara Shikoh deserves a film. In this particular book, the author makes Dara and Aurangzeb the most dramatic and fascinating personalities.

My best regards.

Yours,

Suresh

23/6/76

Dear Suresh,

Yes, I'm rid of my back ailment at last. I would have written earlier, but found your address was not in my book. I had asked Bansi for it, but he hasn't answered my letter yet. I may be coming to Delhi on 1 July for a three-day seminar. I shall stay at Janpath Hotel and I suggest you give me a ring on 1 morning.

I have been escaping into a hotel in the daytime and coming back home in the evenings after twelve hours of solid work on the screenplay. I am back home now with the whole thing blocked out and about half of the fleshing out completed. I reckon it'll take another three/four days to finish the first draft. The final script will now be very close to it, barring a few embellishments. I don't think

3. Abdul Halim Sharar's *Guzeshta Lucknow,* translated as *Lucknow: The Last Phase of an Oriental Culture.*

there'll be time to type it out before I go to Delhi, but [by] the time I get to Bombay around 10 or so, there should be enough copies for you all.

The greatest problem, of course, was to interweave the background and the foreground. I think this has been done most satisfactorily. The particular difficulty here was that the story tended to stay resolutely away from the annexation (which is the whole point of the story), so that one had to find formal means of connecting the two. In the script, now they bear an almost 50:50 relationship. Not only the annexation—which is presented as drama—but the entire Oudh/East India Company relationship has been condensed in a 6/7-minute sequence early on in the script. This not only gives a firm foundation but enhances both the main story and the annexation. Wajid—and therefore Amjad—is now almost as important as Meer and Mirza. Amjad must be persuaded to play, although I should wait until I've spoken to him. His voice in Sholay sounded hoarse; but he may have assumed it especially for the part.

For Mirza's wife, the best actress would be Madhur Jaffrey;[4] I have written to Ismail for her address in New York. It is really only one proper scene, but calls for the whole gamut of acting. Vidya could be hopelessly out of her depth. Meer's wife is a small part which a second stringer could play. We shouldn't offer it to Shabana. We'll think of the casting in Bombay.

Another important part is that of General Outram.

4. Ex-wife of actor Saeed Jaffrey. She starred in many Merchant-Ivory films.

This needs a pukka English actor. In case we can't find one here, I shall write to Lindsay Anderson, who is a close friend of mine. There are many actors in repertory groups in and around London who would jump at the opportunity and work for a reasonable fee. I should warn you that there is one 5/6-minute scene in the film between Outram and his assistant (one of the best scenes in the film) which is in English. All the other scenes involving Outram are either with Wajid or with his minister—where, since Outram didn't know Urdu, his words are translated by an interpreter.

I'm convinced that *The Chess Players* will be a landmark—and a simple film to understand—and not unmanageably expensive. Hoping to see you in Delhi.

Yours,

Manik-da

P.S. I forgot to tell you that a chap called Peter Crouch who is producing a film with Saeed Jaffrey cabled to ask if he could have Saeed in November for his film. I said yes because there's quite a bit of shooting in our film where Mirza and Meer don't appear (the historical bit, all the Wajid scenes, the scenes in the Residency). Besides, there are a couple of scenes between Mirza and his wife. All this—or a chunk of this—we could shoot in November (or even in October—if we are ready).

28 June 1976

Dear Manik-da,

Thanks for your letter. I'm thrilled to read that the screenplay has turned out so much to your satisfaction. Right from the start I've harboured a conviction that *Shatranj Ke Khilari* will be one of the most memorable films of our times.

I'm reaching Delhi on 30 and will see you on 1. Kindly plan on having dinner at my house on 2, and please feel free to call anybody you may want to.

My best regards to you and your family.

Yours,
Suresh

12/7/76

Dear Suresh,

I'm sending you under separate cover 3 copies of the screenplay. Two (the carbons) are meant for Shama[5] and Bansi. Please distribute.

There is adequate material here for a two-hour film, although it may not seem so from a look, or even a cursory reading, of the screenplay. As you will see, actions which

---

5. Shama Zaidi translated Ray's original English dialogues into Hindi/Urdu and also designed the costumes for *Shatranj Ke Khilari*. She later went on to become a scriptwriter for many 'new wave' Hindi films.

will be spread over a minute or even a couple of minutes are often described in single sentences. The description of the historical background is extremely terse in the screenplay, although there is considerable footage here. The Kathak and the rahas[6] will together take up about 6/7 minutes. Also, some of the scenes—particularly those involving Meer and Mirza—will be fleshed out with more dialogue and action. But the structure will remain as it is. The treatment, therefore, is perfectly adequate for budgeting, as also for casting, scouting locations, for Shama (costumes) and for Bansi (sets). We can draw up a shooting schedule when I come to Bombay on 24. We have to arrive there on a weekend for the convenience of the Ghoshals,[7] and 17 is too early for me.

As you will see, Wajid is a most important part and carries considerable weight. You must arrange for Amjad to see me as soon as I get to Bombay.

I'm still not 100 per cent happy about Shabana in the role of Mirza's wife. She's too young and well-endowed not to be able to 'rouse' Mirza in the crucial scene. Madhur would certainly be more convincing here. We shall discuss this further in Bombay.

Since the dialogue invariably undergoes small changes at the time of preparing the shooting script, Shama mustn't worry about translation at this stage.

Tell Shama and Bansi that by the time I leave for

---

6. Rahas or ras: a theatrical representation of the dances of Krishna and the gopis.

7. Close relatives of the Ray family, with whom he often stayed.

Bombay, more copies of the script will be ready and their carbons will be replaced with more durable versions.

I hope all is well with you. How's Tinnu?

Yours,

Manik-da

P.S. I hope you realize the need for keeping the treatment absolutely confidential at this stage.

New Delhi

14 July 1976

My dear Manik-da,

I am leaving for Bombay on 16 morning.

I tried to contact Birju Maharaj.[8] He was away to Lucknow and is expected around 18 or so. Anyway, I had a long talk with Mr Gopa Das, the director of the Kathak Kendra, and he felt Birju Maharaj will be able to give us most of the information on dance and music that we need. It might be a good idea if you write to Birju Maharaj asking him the details of the information you need so that during your meeting with him he can have it ready.

The military expert, Mr Gayatri Nath Pant, is out of India on a lecture tour. So far I have not been able to find

---

8. The most renowned exponent of the classical Indian dance form called Kathak. He choreographed the dances and also sang one of the songs in the film.

out when he is due to return. Nobody at the museum[9] seems to know.

By the time this reaches you I will be in Bombay and you can contact me there.

My best regards to you and your family.

Yours sincerely,

Suresh

17/7/76

Dear Suresh,

I assume you will have reached Bombay by now. I'm coming on 24. Since the Ghoshals' new apartment is both much smaller than the last one and out of the way (Cuffe Parade) for you all, I feel it would be convenient if I stayed at Shalimar Hotel. Could you book a double room (with single occupancy) for five days for me from 24? I'm afraid I have to be back in Calcutta on 29. I think five days will be adequate for the work that we have to do at this stage. Apart from broad discussions on the script, we have to:

Talk to Amjad
Decide on the rest of the casting
Draw up a tentative schedule
Budget
Fix up studio
Fix up lab
Fix up two assistants for me

---

9. The National Museum in New Delhi.

Another trip to Lucknow is obviously called for at some time. This time both Bansi and Shama should be with us, and we should—apart from scouting exteriors—be in a position to look at some interiors. If Birju Maharaj could then be contacted in Lucknow, it could save us a trip to Delhi.

Have you written to Amrit Rai[10] yet? It's time the rights were bought.

Best,

Yours,

Manik-da

19 July 1976

Dear Manik-da,

Thanks for your letter and the scripts which were awaiting my arrival in Bombay. I have given the respective copies to Shama and Bansi-da and we are all naturally thrilled.

I am arranging for your stay at Shalimar Hotel. There's no problem there.

I have already talked to Surinder Suri and Kamal Swaroop about assisting you. However, I have made it very clear that the final decision rests with you. Mr Suri was extremely keen, and I took the liberty of informing him about your apprehension that since he has been directing his own movies, he may not want to assist. But

---

10. The son of Premchand, himself a prominent Hindi writer.

he seems very keen on it. And, personally, he struck me as a serious person.

Unfortunately, I do not have Mr Amrit Rai's address. I hope I can get it prior to your arrival.

You will be happy to know that my uncle[11] has taken *Shatranj Ke Khilari* for Bengal, Delhi-UP and Punjab. I am hoping Rajshri[12] will take the rest of the Indian territories.

More later.

Regards,

Suresh

~

Ray had wanted Bombay-based assistants, since initially the filming was to be done there. He had asked me to suggest some names and I recommended the ones mentioned in the above letter. When it was decided that filming would be done in Calcutta instead, he decided to use his regular (Bengali) assistants. This being a non-Bengali film, Ray felt he needed constant help to check the Urdu language used in the film; and thus, Javed Siddiqui, who was initially contracted as a co-translator of dialogues, also became his special assistant. Ray was a perfectionist and wanted all his films to be correct down to the last detail in order to be absolutely believable to the audience.

---

11. A major film distributor.

12. India's largest production, distribution and exhibition company at the time.

3/8/76

Dear Suresh,

A fat envelope from Saeed Jaffrey with some excellent photographs and a long letter [arrived]. I had asked him about remuneration, to which he replies as follows:

'I don't know how to approach this subject but, as you know, all contracts have to go through my agent here: Peter Crouch Ltd, London. All I can say is that he is not greedy and grasping, and he is as thrilled as I am at the prospect of working with you, and he is conversant with foreign exchange problems. But would you like to write a confirming letter with details of employment, fare, expenses, etc.?'

I think it would be a good idea if at this point you take over from me. I'm going to write to Saeed today and tell him to expect to hear from you.

Also, Saeed asks if we need his measurements. Shama could advise you on this.

I shall start on the shooting script in about a week's time. I have written to Cairo pleading inability to serve as a juror. I shall let you know when I hear from them.

Best,

Manik-da

P.S. Anil babu, my production manager, feels that you ought to come down here one of these days for financial discussions. Let me know when you can make it.

~

After eliminating a few actors and hitting upon the idea that Richard Attenborough, a well-known and highly respected actor knighted by the Queen, would be perfect for the role of Outram, we decided to go to London in the fall of 1976 to meet him, and also to research the costumes of the period at the India Office Library and the Imperial War Museum. We met Richard at the Gaylord Restaurant in Mayfair. Ray and Richard already knew each other from film festivals, and the latter had previously expressed a desire to work with Ray. Richard was at the time editing *A Bridge Too Far*, and it was only due to his enormous respect for Ray that he spared time for us. Perhaps a bit embarrassed to ask such an illustrious actor to play a small role, Manik-da made the offer but added: 'This is not a big role, Richard, but as far as I am concerned you are the only one who can do it.' To which Attenborough immediately replied: 'Satyajit, I would be happy to recite even the telephone directory for you!'

I remember going to Calcutta airport with Ray to meet Richard when he arrived for the shoot. We were discussing the details of a press conference scheduled for the next day for which we still had no moderator, when Manik-da suddenly turned to me: 'Baba, you do it.'

'*Me*, sir? Why, I've never done anything like it! You must remember I was trained as an engineer and not a public speaker. I'm sure I wouldn't know how to handle it.'

'It's not difficult,' was his laconic reply.

'But, sir, the press can be *very* difficult. I wouldn't want to blow it.'

'Oh, it's not at all difficult. All you have to remember is that the press is very stupid, especially here. They never do their homework and then go on to ask all sorts of inane questions about your film. So just tell them anything you want.'

So, overcoming my demons of shyness and feelings of inadequacy, I did exactly that. Of course, the press lapped up everything I said, whether it made sense or not, because I was, in effect, speaking for one of the greatest directors and they were already in awe of him. And they certainly had *not* done their homework and, as I had been warned, asked some pretty dumb questions.

6

Final Preparations

We continued to work towards the shooting of *Shatranj Ke Khilari*, taking care of the innumerable details, consulting one another as well as others, procuring materials, setting up equipment, readying the sets and costumes, and working on translations. Essentially, working tirelessly to make the best Ray film ever: Ray in colour, in Hindi/Urdu, larger than life! My dreams were finally beginning to materialize.

August 3, '76

My dear Manik-da,

I hope everything is well with you.

I have written to Saeed and Amrit Rai and will keep you posted when I hear from them.

IMPPA[1] has allowed the use of *Shatranj Ke Khilari* as the title of the film.

I saw Kiran Shantaram at Rajkamal regarding the use of the studios. Their large floor measures 110 x 60ft wall-to-wall. They only need to be informed thirty days ahead of time.

I met Bansi-da last Sunday. He will be busy most of this month as he has to put up four sets, so I think as of now the trip to Lucknow may not be possible for him this month. He was a little upset that we have planned the shooting from 15 Nov. Anyway, as it was late at night on one of the sets under construction, on which the shooting was to start next morning, he was in a harassed mood. We will be having a meeting under calmer circumstances at the end of this week. He also mentioned that the Rajkamal floors will be small for our purpose. On these matters Bansi-da will be in touch with you directly.

There is a likelihood that the film with Sathyu will be postponed. In that case, I will be making a trip to Calcutta during the third week of this month. In the meantime I will be sticking around in Bombay.

Shama is waiting for the photographs from the Lucknow Museum to start on the costumes.

My best regards to you and the family.

Yours

Suresh

P.S. I hope you will let me know as soon as the actor for Outram is finalized.

---

1. Indian Motion Picture Producers' Association.

August 11, '76

My dear Manik-da,

Thanks for your letter which I have received today.

Sanjeev is in town and I had a meeting with him yesterday to settle his remuneration. Everything is well. He will be in Bombay until 26.

Met Amjad also and gave him his part of the script. I will be giving Sanjeev the script for a day on 15 August—it being a holiday for the industry also.

I have not yet received a reply to my letter to Shri Amrit Rai.[2] In my letter to him I did not make any offer for price but asked him to quote. As suggested by you, we can easily afford to pay Rs 15,000 or even a little more if you feel it necessary.

I can be in Calcutta on or before 20 August and will let you know the exact date of my arrival.

Bansi-da was over for dinner last Monday; asked him for a budget for the sets and he feels it's difficult unless he knows the details of what the interiors require.

Shama is working on the translation of the dialogues.

The photos from the museum[3] have not yet arrived. I have written to Mr Kunwar Narain[4] to pursue the matter.

My best regards and wishes for your well-being.

Suresh

---

2. About the story rights.

3. Lucknow Museum.

4. A renowned Hindi poet.

August 16, '76

My dear Manik-da,

Bansi-da and I are reaching Calcutta on 19 afternoon.

I have received a letter from Saeed Jaffrey's agents, a copy of which I am enclosing for your perusal.

Bansi-da is coming along, as he is likely to be busy with his sets during your sojourn in Bombay. I feel we can have a good discussion in Calcutta regarding the sets, as that is still the one matter of considerable worry.

My best regards to you and your family.

Yours sincerely,

Suresh

Dear Suresh,

I had a talk with Anil Babu,[5] and he feels as strongly as I do that you must come down to Calcutta in the near future for a discussion. As you suggest, 3rd week of August should be all right.

I have written to Lindsay re: Outram, and to Amrit about the rights. I don't think you should offer less than fifteen.

I should be free from my other commitments in about a week's time, and then plunge straight into the shooting script.

---

5. Anil Choudhury, the production manager.

A letter from Dr Narayana Menon[6] suggests that I may have to come to Bombay for a couple of days in the last week of August. Mangesh[7] has seen the documentary on Bala and feels the mixing can be improved (he was away when the job was done). Also there's a possibility of the commentary being recorded again. They did a rather lousy job of recording here in Calcutta.

Perhaps we could fly back together? I have told Narayana that I can come after 23 for a couple of days. If Sanjeev is in town then, we can have a session with him.

Best,

Manik-da

Dear Suresh,

I assume you've got back in Bombay by now. Have just received a telegram from Saeed as follows:

'Completely understand situation. Now awaiting Suresh's letter. Agent on our side. No problem, rest assured.'

I saw the GOC[8] of the Eastern Command, Jacobs,[9]

---

6. Director of the National Centre for the Performing Arts in Bombay. He commissioned the documentary on Balasaraswati that Ray had been working on.

7. Mangesh Desai, a wizard at re-recording and mixing at Rajkamal Studios. Ray would not let anyone else do the sound-mixing of his films.

8. General Officer Commanding: an army general in charge of a command area.

9. J.F.R. Jacob

Satyajit Ray in his study at home in Calcutta

Dalhousie: Letters

1857 "The wreck at Lucknow, why they sent his Crown to the Exhibition, must have been his trouble and in a front service if he thus kept his best 'n'it : & he knew would have missed it. That is a cheese... he will drop into our mouths one day. It has long been missing ; but in these days assassination is in importance. The Charter Committee is to hear, that I feel sure the Court would approve of my sharing the trip help of them."

"The King if Oude seemed disposed to be troublesome : I wish he would to... swallow... bequest to so... into for him... satisfied in..."

1855 "... I should mind doing it as a parting coup : but I meet the people at home having the pluck to sanction it, & if can't print a protest for doing it without a sanction. The King won't offer an ... with us, & sole take any amount of... nothing being rebellion ..."

London, March 24, 58

"Two brigades to proceed to Lucknow. The first commanded by Colonel Wheeler consisted of the Napoleons S.C.H., two batteries, little ones, & the 1st Light Cavalry, a battery of Artillery, & 1st, 2nd, 3rd Native Infantry. The second of the... irregular cavalry, a battery of Artillery, & the 22nd & 44th Native Infantry."

from Bourjois, photograph

Low native Gentleman have... have chairs, Other man wha, other were not permitted to sit in the presence of the ... of the ... whether stood whilst others received an similar spell.

My suspicion was Rhaotney Surgeon, ... of the King's household, & Court Martin, & I am also in mutual charge of the Mauritius school.

[right margin] The Residency was carried from the terrace in a... Terraces into the Durbar room be tried he consulted in a small antechamber to the entrance of... Hall... The Residency appear, without his chair, the King... Minister at the Door, & having... chair, which done with his palm Who walked into an inner room thus... The Minister with King's right hand sat the King's door while amongst the former Prince to the... Members united, standing.

OUTRAM 281

Conquest of Scinde

"Everything has been distributed to those concerned in the War : Colonel Outram, though a brave man, would not take money which he did not think he thought his, & has refused to enrich himself by ill gotten gains."
— Goldsmid II
(quoting Lady Lawrence)

1857 "I have been at my desk ever morning (when I returned from my ride), till 9 (when I breakfast & dress), breakfast over has half past, & again at the desk till half past 5, leaving... really, riding up to Dinner time at 7 o'clock."
He said no complaint of this — quoth the Century.

Such occupation, he declared, agreed with him better. "from the greatest exercise out of ... & he was never better." but he believes the smaller forms & contrivances & minor vexations of his office, would have harassed many to have left away from a place. the petty peppering duties of which 'he found so 'dissatisfied' and the climate 'so disgraceful'

"The morning drive he understood as a necessary penance.
... though by dint of much persuasion he had been led to purchase a tidy horse, he felt it was at... quite another matter, the... hard to have... ."

Outram (cont.) 282

"His forehead is broad, massive, square but open; his eye, whilst in normal state, lazy grey, is dull, only... penetration ; quiet & expressive; his coarse, natural the feeling ; his speech is marked by a slight hesitation when choosing a word, but it is singularly correct & forcible; in his smile & very... & sympathetic.

He is of the middle size, & very strongly built, & has a slight soupçon of the Pharisee, except for the... in application of the field."

1862 "The... humour, his often... of the Pharisees, his many... added to the ... of the well bred & well timed anecdote, & he had no peculiar way of looking again & laughing with his eyes to which... from... would to he pleasant comments in shy smiles.

He had no fine... , without... arts to the profession, & he... appreciated music of a touching character. Sacred music, always his preference."

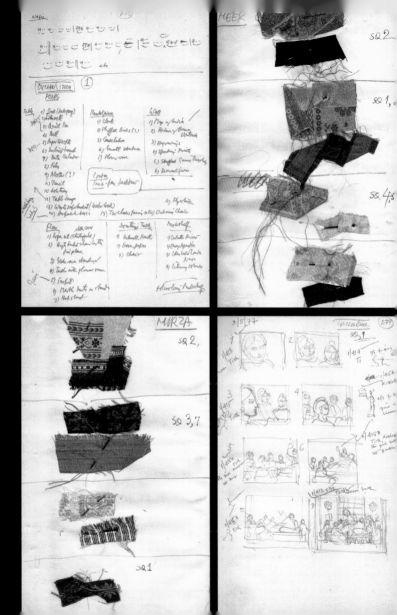

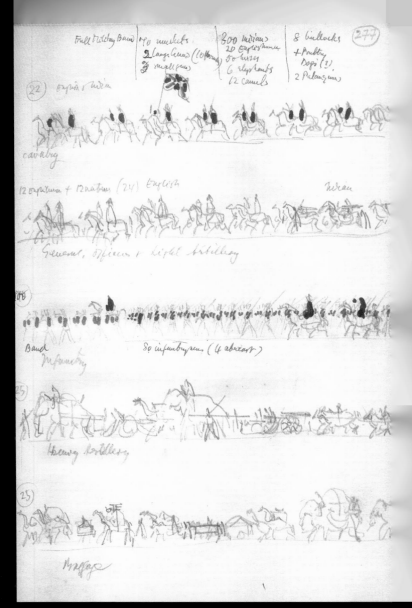

Pages from Ray's cloth-bound shooting notebooks (kheror khata) for *Shatranj Ke Khilari*, including historical notes on characters, fabric samples for costumes, sketches of characters/scenes with dialogue, illustrated shooting script and music score.

After his historic portrayal of the macho, ruthless dacoit Gabbar Singh in *Sholay*, Amjad Khan was a revelation as the effeminate, music-loving nawab Wajid Ali Shah

Wajid Ali Shah (Amjad Khan) with Prime Minister Ali Naqi Khan (Victor Banerjee)

Wajid Ali Shah (Amjad Khan) in his harem

Wajid Ali Shah (Amjad Khan) plays Lord Krishna in *Rahas*, a drama written by Wajid

Wajid Ali Shah (Amjad Khan) with General Outram
(Richard Attenborough) in court

Wajid Ali Shah (Amjad Khan) abdicates by offering his crown to General
Outram (Richard Attenborough), who is attended by Captain Weston
(Tom Alter)

General Outram (Richard Attenborough) in his study

Doctor Joseph Fayrer
(Barry John)

Meer Roshan Ali (Saeed Jaffrey)
and Mirza Sajjad Ali (Sanjeev Kumar)

Meer Roshan Ali (Saeed Jaffrey), Mirza Sajjad Ali (Sanjeev Kumar) and Bookie (Kamu Mukherjee)

Meer Roshan Ali (Saeed Jaffrey) and Mirza Sajjad Ali (Sanjeev Kumar) plan their moves

Mirza Sajjad Ali (Sanjeev Kumar) with Khurshid (Shabana Azmi)

Khurshid (Shabana Azmi)

Aqil (Farooq Sheikh)

Nafeesa (Farida Jalal) with Aqil (Farooq Sheikh)

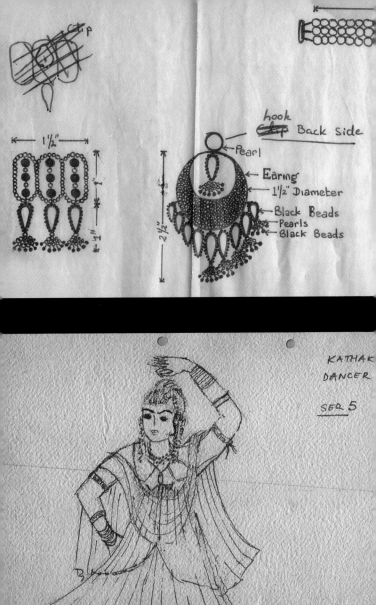

Clip

hook ~~clip~~ Back side

Pearl

← Earing

1½" Diameter

Black Beads
Pearls
Black Beads

1½"

1"

½"

2½"

KATHAK
DANCER

SER 5

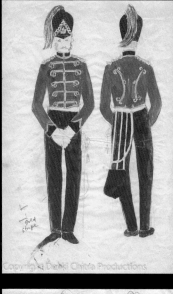

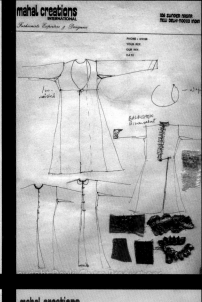

mahal creations
INTERNATIONAL
Fashionists Exporters & Designers

106 SUNDER NAGAR
NEW DELHI-110003 INDIA

PHONE : 618138
YOUR REF.
OUR REF.
DATE

low-waisted

BALKISHEN
Brown velvet

12 large button
in front
6 on sleeve
2 inch-wide
gold stripe

hooks

coat

mahal creations
INTERNATIONAL
Fashionists Exporters & Designers

106 SUNDER NAGAR
NEW DELHI-110003 INDIA

PHONE : 618138
YOUR REF.
OUR REF.
DATE

for uniform

As Sample

BANIA
TYPE

PATTI

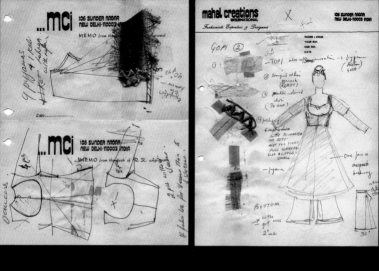
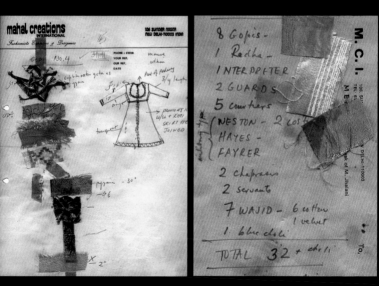

Costume sketches by Manju Raj Saraogi

Jewelled ornaments worn by
actors, including armband,
pair of shoes embellished with
pearls, and royal crown

Ray (behind camera) and team prepare a shot with Richard Attenborough (General Outram) and Tom Alter (Captain Weston)

Ray with Richard Attenborough (General Outram)

Ray rehearses Farida Jalal (Nafeesa) and Farooq Sheikh (Aqil) with Saeed Jaffrey (Meer Roshan Ali) (back to camera)

Ray rehearses with Shabana Azmi (Khurshid) and Sanjeev Kumar (Mirza Sajjad Ali)

Ray with dialogue assistant and wardrobe designer Shama Zaidi

Ray with Veena (Aulea Begum, Queen Mother)

Ray with Samarth Narain (Kalloo)

Ray with lighting cameraman Soumendu Roy (centre) and Roy's assistant

Ray with art director
Bansi Chandragupta,
sound recordist Narinder
Singh (in front of pillar)
and team

Ray with dialogue assistant Javed Siddiqui and team

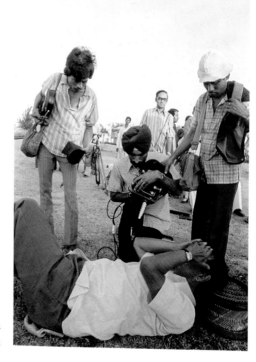

Ray demonstrates a
camera position

Ray as camera operator

Ray frames a shot with camera crew

Amjad Khan (Wajid Ali Shah) with dance director Birju Maharaj (right) and others, including Sandip Ray (centre)

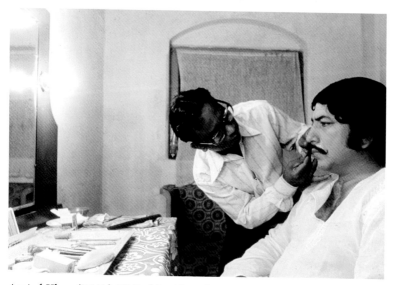

Amjad Khan (Wajid Ali Shah) with make-up artist Ananta Das

Shabana Azmi (Khurshid) and Sanjeev Kumar (Mirza Sajjad Ali) with dialogue assistant Javed Siddiqui (centre)

Suresh Jindal with Sanjeev Kumar (Mirza Sajjad Ali)

Ray with Richard Attenborough (General Outram)

Ray with Suresh Jindal

Ray with Richard Attenborough and Suresh Jindal

SATYAJIT RAY'S

SHATRANJ KE KHILARI

THE CHESS PLAYERS

EASTMANCO

A DEVKI CHITRA
PRODUCTION

FROM THE STORY B
PREMCHAND

PRODUCED BY
SURESH JINDAL

A FILM BY
SATYAJIT RAY
FROM A STORY
BY PREMCHAND
PRODUCED BY
SURESH JINDAL

SHATRANJ
KE KHILARI

THE CHESS PLAYERS

EASTMANCOLOR
BY GEMINI

A DEVKI CHITRA PRODUCTION

Sketch from final pages of Ray's shooting notebooks for
Shatranj Ke Khilari

yesterday at Fort William. He was extremely helpful and went to the extent of lending me 2 rare books on army costumes—one of which is very useful. Unfortunately they have no museum here, and he doesn't know of a place where costumes of that period would be on display. There's nothing in Barrackpore. Jacobs took me to his house in Alipur where I saw a silver hookah from Murshidabad. A magnificent piece which I hope he will lend us for our film. I haven't come to the point where I can ask him to loan it to us; but I mean to cultivate him a little more, and have hope of succeeding.

I'm preparing a shooting schedule which I will send you in a day or two.

For Rammohan[10]—for the animation re: Cherry—I have decided to restrict myself only to the Dalhousie period. This means the following states and titular heads:

1848 - SATARA (Shahuji Raja)

'49 - PUNJAB (Dilip Singh)

'52 - BURMA (King Pengan Meng)

'53 - JHANSI (Raja Gangadhar Rao)

'54 - NAGPUR (Raghuji Bhonsla)

'55 - KARNATAK

(Nawab Ghulam Md. Ghaus Khan)

I'll be on the lookout for the portraits concerned, but I should like enquiries to be made in Bombay also.

On page 144–45 in *The Mussalmans of India*, there is a useful description of the throne of Oudh. Please refer

10. Ram Mohan: one of India's pioneering and leading animation artists. He worked on the film.

Bansi to it. I'm producing a sketch on the basis of it as well as the Ghazi-ud-din portrait in Victoria Memorial. I'm also proceeding with the other sketches.

Incidentally, Jacobs told me how an army marching into Lucknow would be arranged. The order is this:

1) Scouts 2) Cavalry 3) Horse artillery (light) 4) General and staff 5) Infantry 6) Heavy artillery (bullocks or elephants) 7) Baggage

Horses, therefore, are a must. He said Delhi was the likeliest place for them.

I am still feeling hesitant about offering Nafeesa's role to Shabana. If at all, she should play Khurshid. Since I didn't talk to Tanuja[11] personally, I don't feel obliged to give her a part. Judging by her looks, I think Farida Jalal[12] would be a good choice for Nafeesa. She has the impish look, and I believe she's not a bad actress (Babu has seen her in several films). I should like you to think this over.

My thumb is swollen again, hence this barely legible scrawl.

I hope Shama has made some progress with the translation.

If you have the Bourne & Shepherd[13] pictures with you, take a look at the one which says 'The vinery and buildings in the Kaiserbagh'. The palace shown in the left

---

11. A Bollywood star at the time.

12. A young actress whose career was just taking off then. She ended up playing the role of Nafeesa.

13. Bourne & Shepherd (B & S): the second oldest photo studio in the world, based in Calcutta.

doesn't exist any more and may well have been Wajid's own palace because it is also shown in an excellent engraving in my fat book (Rousselet) on the native states. Also take a look at the photo of Kaiserbagh East State and compare it with the picture of the same gate in Sharar's book. You will see how different it looked in pre-Mutiny days. B & S photographed it immediately after the Mutiny and what we see today is what the taluqdars[14] did with it. All the Lucknow photos in Sharar are pre-Mutiny and all come from the India House. I have written to Pam Cullen[15] to send me a complete list of what they've got on Lucknow.

Best wishes.

Yours,

Manik-da

14 September 1976

My dear Manik-da,

I am leaving for Bombay this evening. Was planning to come back to Delhi by the 18 but since, according to my information, the National Film Awards have been postponed to mid-October, my programme is flexible.

---

14. Feudal landholders whom the British co-opted after 1857.

15. A friend, who was an officer at the Indian embassy in London. She was awarded the Padma Shri by the Government of India. She was the 'godmother' of all film-makers, writers and other cultural pros who were looking for connections in England. A wonderfully helpful and well-loved woman.

I have spoken to Dr Pant, the military expert at the National Museum. He is most helpful and will do all the research for us, including weapons and uniforms.

The treaty between Wajid and the East India Company is in the National Archives and they will cooperate with us fully.

Shama has discovered that the actual costumes used by Wajid for the rahas are in a mandir in Vrindavan. A very interesting detail: Wajid gave the funds for the construction of the temple. I will go there when I next come to Delhi.

B/W photos of the Mahmoodabad Palace will be sent to you by Saturday. The colour prints will have to be made in Bombay, and we only get the negatives on Wednesday (15).

The Lucknow Museum authorities were very helpful. The additional director of cultural affairs in UP is a personal friend of Mr Kunwar Narain, and he came with us to the museum. We discovered a series of 28 drawings of 'Wajid and his Pastimes' by some court painter. You will be amused to know that a drawing of the incident related by Bansi-da, where a begum lassoed another one with a whip in the Pari Khana, is also there. We have photographed them all and will send you a copy. It might be of interest to you to put them in your proposed book.

I met Birju Maharaj today. I have told him what all we want done, particularly mentioning that the exact details will be given by you. His Ram Lila is to be staged on 10, 11 and 12 December.

In case the National Film Awards are postponed, it

may be a good idea for you to come to Delhi sometime this month for discussing details with Birju Maharaj and Dr Pant. I will telephone you to find out your programme.

Regards.

Yours sincerely,

Suresh

September 17, '76

My dear Manik-da,

Enclosed here are the photos of the interior of the Mahmoodabad Palace.

Met Shabana today. She will be glad to do the role. She'll be here in Bombay when you come, so you can talk to her directly.

I have managed to locate at least one carpet (about 30x30ft) for our set. It's a patterned Mirzapuri, which I think will serve our purpose. A lot of silver knick-knacks are also available.

Sanjeev's secretary may be able to get a bungalow for your stay at Juhu. I will be seeing it on Monday.

Regards,

Suresh

17/9/76

Dear Suresh,

I'm enclosing the shooting chart. You can now easily work out the number of days the main actors will be needed for, and also find out the dates on which they will be required. Don't show this chart to Bansi yet, or he'll throw up his hands again. The right psychological moment is after I've handed in the designs for the sets. I'm sketching them in great detail, including measurements, plans, elevations, etc. Bansi will only have to get them executed. Bansi told me he's not free in September. Find out from him if he's absolutely free from October for 3 months at a stretch. If not, then I'll definitely take on Ashok as associate art director.

The Ghoshals have decided to keep their Cuffe Parade flat so that we can go and stay there. This is a big load off our minds, as well as yours. Since this will call for Gopa's presence in Bombay to run the household, you'll have to pay for her passage. Plus, we could work out a sum which you could pay for monthly expenses. I think this could work out to be a third of what it would have cost to stay in a rented flat, and a fourth of what it would have cost in a hotel.

The director of Orient Longman dropped in yesterday. He is a south Indian from Hyderabad. One of the leading families there. He invited me to come and look at his antiques (his grandfather was given a sword by the viceroy which we will certainly need). He says he will let us use anything that we find suitable, free of charge. Have managed to get two splendid shawls—almost museum pieces—which would do for Meer and Mirza.

I'm sorry! Still have a swollen thumb. It makes writing difficult (I can sketch though).

I hope to see you in Bombay in a week or so; will phone you when I've fixed the date. I hope Shama is working on the dialogues.

Yours,

Manik-da

23/9/76

Dear Suresh,

After talking to you on the phone last night I've been thinking about our production, and the following have occurred to me:

We must think of an alternative translator; Shama can't possibly cope with two things.[16] The only writers I know personally in Bombay are Inder and Gulzar.[17] Bansi says Inder doesn't know Lucknow's Urdu. Check on this: Is Gulzar capable of handling the job? Perhaps he's too busy. Please find out.

There are all sorts of props, textiles, etc., still available in Calcutta. In most cases the owners are prepared to

---

16. Translation and costumes.

17. Inder: Inder Raj Anand, writer/director. Gulzar: well-known writer, director, lyricist and poet.

lend them to us provided they are being used in Calcutta. Since I don't see how the film can be made without such props—and since there is small chance of getting similar stuff in Bombay—I think we should seriously consider the implications of shooting in Calcutta. The Indrapuri floors are larger than Rajkamal's. We can hire extra lights if necessary. One snag of course is that we can't see daily rushes; but this is a small price to pay when you think of the other advantages—after including considerable saving on costs. Of the actors, only Sanjeev and Amjad will have to stay in a hotel for long stretches (for Saeed Bombay or Calcutta makes no difference). The others are required only for 2/3 days each. Most of the crew comes from Calcutta; both you and Bansi have places to stay here. Two of the actors—Ali Naqi and Bal Kishen—are from Calcutta. We can get all the non-speaking extras from here.

If we book well in advance, we can get Subrata's[18] equipment for the shooting, which will be better than anything Bombay has to offer. Off hand, I can't think of any serious disadvantages at all. But I'm writing this on the spur of the moment, and I would request you to give the matter serious thought. The songs could be recorded in Bombay. In fact, the rehearsals could take place in Bombay, where only myself and my assistants would be needed.

Gemini has written to me in a vein that suggests that they are prepared to go a long way in accommodating us.

18. Subrata Mitra, the cameraman who shot Ray's first film as well as all subsequent films until *Nayak* (1966).

Their negative developer is still first rate, and I'm sure they'll take extra care on this film.

Do let me know what you feel.

Manik-da

7/11/76

Dear Suresh,

Two or three things which I forgot to mention in our telephone conversations:

Anil Babu's estimate of the first set is about Rs 25,000. He is much more reliable than Bansi, who in any case never produces a budget.

I found a letter from Amrit Rai waiting for me when I returned from Bombay. He fears that we have dropped Shatranj. I think you should arrange to go Allahabad from Delhi and then come to Calcutta.

With all that work to be done in London, don't you think it would simplify matters if I were to hop over for a couple of days at least before we start shooting? Jana Aranya is showing at Teheran and I found a two-way ticket waiting for me at SAS [South Asian Society]. Perhaps I could use that ticket, fly over to London from Teheran and come back before Sanjeev and Saeed arrive in Calcutta. I could arrange to go to Teheran from Bombay, spend a couple of days there and then carry on to London[19]— provided work on the site in Calcutta has progressed

19. Eventually, he did not go to Teheran, only to London.

to a point where my presence is no longer necessary. I could myself photograph the throne, the war costumes, Dalhousie's letter and the Crystal Palace poster, as well as talk to Gerald James,[20] or even James Mason[21]—if he doesn't ask for an exorbitant fee. It really depends on whether you can find room for my trip in your budget. Just think about it.

Yours,
Manik-da

13/5/77

Dear Suresh,

I've just had a letter from Marie Seton.[22] It seems that she has been entrusted with the job of bringing Attenborough's costumes. She was under the impression that we were shooting in Bombay, but I have sent her a cable and informed her of the change of venue. She will stay through the shooting and do a couple of pieces for London papers. I took the liberty of offering her hospitality on your behalf. Apparently the costumes have to come as personal baggage, and Attenborough being away, Pam Cullen was left with no choice but to rope in Marie.

---

20. British actor.

21. Internationally famous British actor.

22. British writer, known for her biographies of Ray and Eisenstein.

1) Military Costumes:

I'll send Maya[23] a colour sample as soon as I receive Mollo's[24] drawings from Bombay. Till yesterday they hadn't arrived. The front line costumes can be made in Calcutta. If the powder blue of the sepoys' trousers is really light, we can use them in place of white. In sunlight they'll look lighter still.

Shama must send me Barry John's measurements immediately if Fayrer's costumes are to be made in Calcutta. Incidentally, although I have a lock of John's hair and his photograph, I still don't have his address. I want to drop him a line before he shows up here. I've had no communication with him at all except a few words at your party in New Delhi.

The more I think about it, the more I feel that Weston,[25] too, should be wearing civilian clothes in Outram's office. After all he too had a political job as Outram's assistant. At any rate, let me have Weston's measurements too. In the meantime I'll make a few enquiries and come to a final decision on this. I don't see Weston wearing knee-high boots at any time. The levee uniform would call for ordinary military boots and black trousers with bands.

As for Fayrer's and Outram's shoes, they can wear their own since the feet won't be seen. Same for Weston.

---

23. Ray is referring to Manju Raj Saraogi, who fabricated the costumes for the film.

24. Andrew Mollo, an expert on military costumes. He drew the sketches for the film's costumes.

25. Aide of General Outram, played by Tom Alter.

I hope Shama has noted the fact that a bearer appears in Outram's study. In case she hasn't, she must let me know immediately. I'm sure this will have to be a special dress which I can check on and have made in Calcutta.

2) Advertisements:

In general, I agree with your views, and I'm instructing Zehra[26] accordingly. *Shatranj* is a tough proposition adwise because of the multiplicity of themes in the film. One has to choose between so many alternatives. Zehra's approach is cool, sophisticated, elegant and abstract. What she needs is an infusion of heart and a consideration for the 99% of the film's potential audience who will not respond to her kind of approach. It is possible—and I'm going to send her some ideas—to produce more pictorial, storytelling ads within the norms of good taste. One has to go more for ideas and human interest than for patterns and textures.

Women—at least Shabana—must be included in the hoardings, and possibly also in the six-sheeters; and I should include both Amjad and Attenborough.

By the way, Zehra tells me that you would like Munshi added to Premchand [in the credits]. I discussed this point with Amrit and he feels as I do—e.g., Premchand being a pen name, it doesn't gain anything by the addition of an honorific. I'm sure Premchand himself would have agreed. The UNESCO collection of his stories is called *The World of Premchand*, and not *The World of Munshi Premchand*.

---

26. Zehra Tyabji, the film's graphic designer.

I sent Javed[27] the new dialogue for the Aulea and Ali Naqi scenes. Veena[28] should have the new version right away. Tom also needs the interpreter dialogues as soon as possible. As we haven't yet gone over those dialogues and can do so only after Shama and Javed are here, I suggest that Tom arrives at least three days before shooting so that he has enough time to learn his lines.

We are now busy looking for props. Ashok[29] feels confident that he can finish all three sets in time.

Best

Yours,

Manik-da

P.S. I think August 12 is too soon for the release. I shall need two clear months for final cut, music (composing and recording), laying the tracks, and mixing. Soumendu[30] will need a week at least for grading and then a week more for the prints to come out. Also, we must make every effort to get the dissolves done abroad. Mid-September would be OK.

~

---

27. Javed Siddiqui, who translated the dialogues with Shama Zaidi. It was his first film job. He went on to become a highly successful Bollywood writer.

28. A famous actress from India's silent movie era who played the role of the king's mother.

29. Ashok Bose, the associate art director.

30. Soumendu Roy, the cameraman.

For the costumes referred to in these letters, the attire of the period was thoroughly researched by Ray, and then Andrew Mollo was hired to draw the sketches for the costumes. Andrew is the younger brother of John Mollo, two-time Oscar winner for costume design in *Star Wars* and *Gandhi*. Much to our dismay, Andrew's wonderful sketches for *Shatranj Ke Khilari* were later lost or stolen, and hence could not be included in this book.

As for the translations, Ray wrote his original screenplay dialogues in English and many people were considered for the translation—as is reflected in the letters—but eventually Javed Siddiqui and Shama Zaidi translated them from English to Urdu/Hindi. Ray wrote all his film dialogues in Bengali. His English was also impeccable, but his knowledge of Hindi and Urdu was minimal. *Shatranj Ke Khilari*'s dialogues were translated into Urdu/Hindi and Awadhi, the local dialect of the Awadh region, of which Lucknow was the capital. In the film, the aristocrats speak Urdu among themselves, but when addressing the domestic staff they speak Awadhi.

7

Filming

♟♟♟♟♟♟

We started filming in December 1976 and finished in June 1977. It took sixty-seven days to complete the principal photography.[1] All interiors were filmed at Indrapuri Studios in Calcutta and the exteriors in various parts of Lucknow, a small village near Lucknow and Jaipur.

A Ray film was solely *his* film: He wrote it, directed it, operated the camera (even if he had a designated cameraman), edited it, composed the music and designed the sets and the publicity materials. He never said this out loud, but those around him knew it without being told. Despite this, he was good at delegating work and was profusely grateful for loyalty and hard work. But perhaps the best quality about him was how he always

---

1. There was no second-unit work.

encouraged others and was extremely patient. He never made anyone feel small or insignificant, though his very presence—towering personality, height and booming voice—could be overwhelming to say the least. He was also a superb manager with an uncanny sense of what could be delegated and who was best for the job.

Ray was truly a Renaissance man. There seemed to be nothing that he could not do. And he was also disciplined, at his desk from morning until night, when not filming, writing a children's book (which he did every year), composing music, writing screenplays and making illustrations.

The main visualizations and sketches of the sets of *Shatranj Ke Khilari* were done by Ray. Bansi Chandragupta, his friend and art director from the beginning of his career, who had moved to Bombay a decade earlier, did the art direction again, and was given quite a bit of autonomy since Ray trusted him implicitly to carry out his vision.

We didn't have the luxury of watching 'dailies' when we filmed in those days. In India, we had to depend on karma, gods, numerologists, astrologers and voodoo men for our daily filming to produce good results. (Not really.) A bit of humour aside, it was hard to know how things had turned out on a daily basis: what the sets looked like, how the actors had performed, etc. But luckily on a Ray film shoot, all that information was stored in that great creative mind. Once he looked through that lens and ran the film, he knew exactly what he had captured in each moment, every day.

I recall an incident about sets and continuity. Upon developing the film, it was discovered that in one shot an actor was without his scarf, which had been part of his costume in earlier shots. Ray, who was most considerate towards his producers, asked me if he could reshoot the scene. Even though I dreaded the expenditure of rebuilding the set, I readily agreed. A day later, he called and said he didn't need the whole set, just one wall of it. Gratitude welled up inside me, but I told him that Bansi-da had insisted that the whole set be rebuilt.

'Don't bother about Bansi. You see, Suresh, all art directors always want elaborate sets so that they can be admired by all who see the film. We can do it with just one background wall,' was his considerate response.

Ray's first cinematographer, Subrata Mitra, whose work is taught in film schools around the world, fell out with him because Ray wanted to operate the camera himself, leaving little room for Subrata to manoeuvre. After his departure, Ray operated the camera himself. Of course, he needed help with the complex business of setting up the shots, lighting, getting the equipment ready for filming, so Soumendu Roy became his cinematographer, making sure all Ray had to do was get behind the camera and shoot.

While filming, the sets had the serenity of an ashram. There was no confusion, lack of discipline or tantrums. There were no unexpected glitches. Always calm and soft-spoken, Ray engendered enormous respect and obedience as a director. His capacity for focus and creativity on the sets was fathomless, inspiring the crew and the actors to deliver the same. And he was never late. Without his ever insisting on it, no one else was late either—a delight for any producer with eyes always on the budget. Of course, he was human and occasionally got upset, but seldom in public. He mostly expressed his anguish and anger behind closed doors to people he trusted.

If he didn't like the way an actor had given a shot, he never said so directly. Instead, this is what usually transpired:

'Rai,[2] was the lighting okay?'

'Yes, Dada.'

'Narinder,[3] was the dialogue okay?'

'Yes, Dada.'

'Good, good,' he would assure the actor, 'but will you please do another take for me?'

And the actors were more than happy to do so.

---

2. Soumendu Roy. Roy is an English corruption of 'Rai', which was his real name, as was Ray's.

3. Narinder Singh, the sound director.

From a long career of low-budget art films, Ray had learnt to make do with very few takes. Generally, every scene was well thought-out and ready to shoot with almost no rehearsal, so that the spontaneity would lend more realism. *Shatranj Ke Khilari*'s cast of professional actors required very few takes anyway. Moreover, Ray had written to each actor ahead of time, explaining the role and how he envisioned it. During the shoot, he outlined the scene, along with the preceding and following ones. When necessary, he would enact the part for a child or a cast member with limited experience. He controlled the rhythm and tenor of the dialogues, which brought out the best in each actor. And even though all decisions were made by him, he kept his ego out of the process; if someone came up with a better suggestion, he was open to it (although it was difficult to come up with something better than what he had already thought of).

Manik-da was always flexible about letting actors add their own touch to a scene. While researching his part as General Outram, Richard Attenborough found that the man smoked cheroots and wore a pince-nez. He thus not only began practising a Scottish accent but also brought the props with him. On arriving at Calcutta airport, he shared these details with Ray at the baggage claim, but quickly added, 'Satyajit, you are the director, and I will do whatever you want.' Ray's immediate response was that if that were the research he would gladly go along with it.

Richard was incredibly pleased at being allowed to bring a depth to his role that he had discovered himself. And when Saeed Jaffrey wanted to deliver certain dialogues in a particular way, knowing that Saeed knew Urdu better than himself, Ray let him.

Usually, other than the night shoots, Ray liked to work from 9 a.m. to 6 p.m., with a one-hour lunch break. Since film shooting involves hard physical labour, especially for the crew, the meal service was substantial. It would usually include heaps of rice, chapattis, dal, at least two vegetables, one non-vegetarian dish, salad and dessert along with tea and coffee. But having already had a large breakfast at home, Ray preferred a light lunch, usually consisting of a sandwich, some sweetmeats, tea and his beloved cigarettes. I noticed that he never ate fruit. He didn't like fruit at all. And he never touched any kind of alcohol either.

Ray usually ate on one side of the set with his son and wife, and any other relative or special visitor that might be visiting on the day. His wife and his son, Sandip, who was his assistant director, accompanied him on all outdoor shoots. He was a complete family man. Considering his prolific and compulsive work habits, that was probably the only way they could get to see enough of him.

When his film unit and the actors were in a mischievous mood, they would affectionately refer to him as God, since he *was* a god of cinema. Of course, they would never dare say this in front of him, only among themselves, but loud enough to be heard by him. One of his assistants had already nicknamed him lambu (tall man). Ray was almost certainly aware of these comments but never let on that he had heard them.

While shooting a film, he would never go out in the evenings, unless it was related to the next day's shoot. He would instead use the time to visualize the following day's scenes or to write dialogues or lyrics (to music he had already composed). Social events made him nervous. Although aware of his stature, he remained a shy and private man. There was a saying: 'If you want to torture Ray take him to a party.' There was no wrap-up party at the end of production.

In his earlier films, Ray had used professional music directors, but since music was one of his many passions and talents he eventually began to score his own films, including *Shatranj Ke Khilari*. Listening to music had always been one of his greatest pleasures and over time he had become equally familiar with Indian and Western music. After he had created a film's score, he clearly communicated his ideas to the musicians and took complete control over directing them, often demonstrating portions on the piano. In Ray's films, his audio tracks—music and effects—are crucial and a joy to study.

But in films, just as in life, things do not always go

smoothly, even in the hands of a master. A series of incidents during the shoot created a volatile situation which ultimately exploded in our faces, mine especially. The first of these occurred one evening in Calcutta at the start of the studio shoot when we invited some senior members of Ray's Bengali crew for drinks and dinner at the New Kenilworth Hotel, where the Bombay crew was staying. During the course of inebriated bonhomie, we started ribbing one another about our respective regional cultures and stereotypes.

There were only three of us from Punjab in the room: a Sikh gentleman, a Punjabi who had lived in Calcutta most of his life and thought of himself as a Bengali and me. Sikhs are the universal butt of jokes across India, which depict them as simpletons with 'all brawn and no brain' and unbridled sexual lust. Often, these jokes are narrated by Sikhs themselves, for besides being known for their agricultural skills and bravery, they also have a riotous sense of humour. We cracked many Sikh jokes. Many jokes were made by the Bengalis about Punjabis and my Bania caste. Banias are demonized as greedy businessmen, while Punjabis are stereotyped as uncouth and uncultured, cheats in business and sex maniacs. Many of the jokes that night reflected all these 'attributes'. The Punjabis retaliated with digs at Bengalis' clannish, effete, emotional and high-strung ways and being the ultimate culture vultures. It was meant to be taken in good spirit;

no malice was intended and there was much laughter all around.

The next day, one of my trusted crew members from Bombay, whom I considered a friend, told an important member of the Bengali crew that I held a low opinion of Bengalis and was prejudiced against them; ergo, I was a regional chauvinist. I was stung by this accusation. Discrimination, prejudice and chauvinism of any kind went against the very essence of my character. What was most unbearable was that, of course, this calumny was carried back to Manik-da, a man I deeply admired, as the truth. For reasons known only to them, a few of the Bengalis along with a couple of my 'friends' from the Bombay crew used this episode—along with other incidents—to create a rift between Manik-da and me.

On the last day of this first shooting schedule in Calcutta, I was told that the cheque (which was to be our payroll) from the distributors would be delayed. I requested the production manager of the film Anil Choudhury to explain to the crew why their pay cheques would be delayed. Unfortunately, he was away on some business and failed to do so. In the evening, my nephew Sunil called to tell me that the crew was demonstrating against me in the studio, calling me names, from a 'bloodsucking Marwari' to a 'cheating Punjabi producer from Bombay', even 'a CIA agent' (because of my American education). I rushed to Ray's flat and explained the reason for the delay in payments. Anil babu, who happened to be there, verified my story. And Ray seemed to accept my explanation.

But all that venom from these people troubled me. That too when they had already been paid four months' salaries without a single shot being filmed, since production had to be postponed due to Sanjeev Kumar's heart attack and Amjad Khan's near-fatal accident.

The next incident happened while we were filming in Lucknow. The only five-star hotel in town was Clarks Avadh, where, going by Indian film industry convention, only the producer, director, stars and heads of departments were to be lodged. All assistants and work crew were put up in another hotel that was approved by Anil Choudhury and Bansi Chandragupta, the senior spokesmen and advisers of Ray's Bengali team. Of the heads of departments, Bansi-da, Shama and Narinder chose to stay at the Clarks, while Anil and Soumendu said they preferred to stay with their crew at the other hotel. However, this was eventually presented to Ray as proof of my partiality towards the Bombay personnel and prejudice against the Bengali ones. Ray, spurred by a fierce loyalty towards his long-time crew, ended up upbraiding me for this since he was unaware of what had transpired.

The first day of what was to be an outdoor shoot in Lucknow saw a heavy downpour of unseasonal rain, cancelling all plans. On the second day, while all of us waited impatiently at the Clarks, there was no sign of the crew who were staying at the other hotel. When they finally arrived, half an hour late, Ray, with suppressed anger, asked them the reason for the delay. The answer: There wasn't sufficient hot water to bathe!

On the next day, when the drama was repeated, Ray lost his cool, which he seldom did, and yelled at them for this lack of discipline. Their retort, delivered with equal force, and accusatory looks in my direction, was that 'the fried eggs were cold and when sent back were delayed in being served at the breakfast table'. Given that he had been misinformed about me, Ray turned to me and thundered: 'THIS IS VERY BAD!'

Unable to bear another unfair attack, especially from Manik-da, I replied with barely suppressed fury: 'It is not my job to fry eggs for your production staff. If they do not like their hotel, let them suggest another one in the same budget and they can move there right away. I will bear the cost of a day's delay if they do not want to shoot today while they move to another hotel.'

This was no easy offer on my part considering a whole day had already been lost to rain. Every single delay, especially on location shoots, plays havoc with already tight budgets, more so on low-budget art films. But I was not going to be bullied by people who were bent on driving a wedge between Ray and me. After all this turmoil, my detractors opted to stay where they were staying because they liked the place!

Except for the ringleaders, most of the crew was gentle and decent, and they individually apologized to me for the unpleasantness. The remaining days went by without further theatrics, and we had a satisfactory shoot.

For the final filming in Jaipur, I booked half of Clarks Amer, another five-star hotel. Along with the entire unit, we also accommodated twenty-five couples from the diplomatic corps in Delhi at the hotel. These couples had volunteered to play the East India Company officers for the scenes depicting the army marching to Lucknow at the end of the film.

Being actively involved in the party circuit in Delhi, I had many friends from the diplomatic corps and was thus allowed to put a notice on the bulletin boards of the US, UK and Australian embassies. In no time word got around, and because of the 'Ray magic' people from the USSR, Poland, Germany and other embassies too were pleading to be cast. I had offered to transport them in luxury air-conditioned buses, stocked with food and drinks, and to bear the hotel costs for the weekend of filming. Since all the distributors' instalment monies had already been exhausted, as well as my own funds, I had to borrow money at inflated 'filmy' rates of 50 per cent per month for the finale of the film, hoping that when the distributors' instalments came in, I would be able to repay the loans.

After the last day of the schedule, the return train journey for the Bengali crew was made only for the following night so that they could spend the day sightseeing and shopping. My nephew Sunil was cashier, accountant and financial controller of the production—a role that made him not too popular. After the personal attacks against me and the rancour expressed against Sunil, I asked him to have minimal contact with the Bengali crew on this last shooting schedule. At about 6 p.m. on the last day he called me from the hotel lobby and, in a frightened voice, said, 'Chacha-ji, I *have* to see you immediately.'

I expected the worst. He came to my suite considerably shaken. While he was trying to apprise me of what had happened, the telephone rang. It was Ray. He said angrily, 'You better come to see me *immediately*!' A mix of fear, anger, defiance and deep trepidation bubbled inside me as I went over to his suite, where three agitated crew members gave me chilling looks while walking out. Ray was fuming and let loose a tirade of non-profane invectives against me (he never cursed or used foul language). I was too stunned to utter a word. After he had had his say, I left without requesting his permission or even looking back and, heading straight to my bedroom, let out a desolate howl of rage and despair.

Sunil, who had remained in my suite, handed me a stiff Scotch. When I could finally get myself to speak I told him to go to the hotel cashier, get the bills for me to sign and order a car to take me to Delhi right away. I had had enough.

As I worked my way through a half-filled bottle of Scotch on the road to Delhi that night, I wallowed in self-pity, asking myself over and over: 'And for what? Nothing but a bloody bill of forty-three rupees!' I replayed the incident over and over in my head: I had authorized all the heads of departments to sign meal bills for their assistants (excluding cigarettes and other extras), which the hotel cashier would send me the next day for a countersignature. Since one of the Calcutta crew members was signing out, he was presented with a bill for ₹43.40. While he was puzzling over this, one of the ringleaders started shouting and abusing the receptionist about the bill. Within minutes a 'cell' was formed to inform Ray about this terrible insult I had heaped on the man.

Usually for low-budget art films, which is what Ray had made up to that point, crew accommodation was a rented bungalow and meals were catered by contract cooks, with a fixed menu and strict timing. But despite my paying more than double their usual salaries, organizing a five-star hotel with unquestioned authority to sign for meals in any restaurant of their choice, often at great personal hardship—my phones were disconnected due to unpaid bills and I could not leave my flat for days because I had no money for petrol—I received no appreciation.

The next morning when Ray found out that I had left for Delhi, he dispatched Marie Seton to talk to my older brother Ramesh—a man of great charm and generosity, with whom she had developed a mutual admiration—hoping that she could get him to persuade me not to quit the film. She even gave him a signed copy of her biography of Ray. Through Ramesh, Marie requested my presence at a meeting to resolve things, but I was too angry and hurt to accept.

I sent Ray a handwritten letter (of which I did not keep a copy) in which I poured my heart out. I also told him I would not be attending the remaining work on the film—some patchwork at a Bombay studio and the final RR. And I did not. It was not out of spite. I simply could not bear to face the vitriol of the crew.

Since I cannot fathom why the Bengali crew members chose to behave the way they did, I can only guess that perhaps they felt insecure and did not want Ray to make any more films away from Calcutta.

Eventually, our misunderstandings were cleared up and our relationship returned to an even keel. I preferred to forget what he said that night. For me, he will always be a guru and a bodhisattva. I realize it takes a superior man to write the first sentence of his next letter to me:

24/6/77

Dear Suresh,

It is most unfortunate that I had to speak to you the way I did in Jaipur the other day. No one is sorrier than I am that matters had to come to a point where a showdown was inevitable. One advantage, I think, is that we know each other a little better now. I have never for a moment doubted your respect and admiration for me. If you had shown a fraction of that feeling towards the members of my team, there would be no problems and no cause for me to complain. It was quite an effort for me in Lucknow to overlook the fact that you chose to put up your sound recordist in the same hotel with me, while you treated my cameraman (arguably one of the finest in India) as an ordinary member of the team. Soumendu was forced to swallow this humiliation at my instigation. I realized then that you are inclined to assess a person by his façade and his lifestyle rather than his intrinsic merit. I'm afraid this is a yardstick which I never apply.

I'm not going to recount for your sake all the humiliation that my crew suffered in Jaipur. I can't imagine that you could be so blasé or so insensitive as to be unaware of them. And yet the work was done. In the circumstances it was an outstanding achievement made possible by the total dedication of the crew. But you showed no appreciation of the fact.

I know you have complained to both Shama and Javed for being 'too chummy with the Bengali crowd'. This is an attitude which is totally alien to me, and it appals me that the person for whom I'm making what may well turn out to be a milestone in Indian cinema should possess this chauvinistic trait.

Yours,
Manik-da

June 30th, '77
Bombay

Dear Manik-da,

Professionals don't quit. The job may defeat them (it won't) or they finish the job (I will do my part). I assure you that there will be no change in my professional attitude until *Shatranj* is successfully released. No degree of 'chauvinistic traits' or 'façade and lifestyle' will come in the way of my getting the best people to do the remainder of the work.

Just continue to smile on me a little, and I'll fight the gods for you. With *Shatranj* I'm doing just that: fighting the established gods of Indian cinema. And as far as I'm concerned, they're not even worth the tin on which they're embossed. The tin may have cutting edges but I feel sure we'll melt it with your fire.

An amazing number of lies and half-truths have been told about me (no! I won't justify myself until you ask me). It seems incredible, but was it never brought to your knowledge that I offered to put up all the chief technicians at Clarks Avadh? Or that Raida had been coaxed by me to come to Bombay at my expense for RR? Or that the single most expensive shopping I did in London was for Raida, and when he offered payment I told him to either return the goods or no payment?

That was the coup-de-grâce in Jaipur—when Raida also believed I'd torture the unit with such vicious meanness for only 43 rupees.

I have lived too long with the terror of my own uncertainties, created by people who somehow hate my guts (why, I can't imagine, since these guts were spilled for the film), to know I don't have such petty traits and have the strength and will to rise above them. You have taught me an awful lot, sir, more than I can ever repay you for, but this one thing I've learnt on my own.

I had seen the hotel the Rajmata recommended, but I wanted to make amends for Lucknow (though I still believe the so-called hardship was merely in three people's minds). And at that stage (Jaipur) I paid 50,000 rupees' interest for every 1 lakh I borrowed. What had happened must've been destined, because it happened for 43 rupees. Bills did come for my signature every day, and I did sign them (this 'justification' has the burden of proof).

I very much look forward to seeing you. I'll be coming on 12 July (for Dossani's[4] inauguration) and earlier if the Bombay end gets organized sooner.

Yours,
Suresh

---

4. Of Dossani Films, the distributor for the territory of Bengal.

7/7/77

Dear Suresh,

If you are really serious about restoring normal relations and seeing the film to a peaceful and successful conclusion, you must arrange for money (Anil babu says at least a lakh) to clear dues in Calcutta. The only tactics Sunil has is to tell Anil babu to 'manage things'. And Anil babu seems to have reached the end of his tether. Apart from the 2 or 3 people and organizations who keep phoning me and robbing me of the peace of mind, without which I can't function as an artist, I believe there are quite a few whom money is owed—even fairly large sums. I don't know if this is the way Hindi films are made, but for me this is a new and most unpleasant experience. Mr Dossani came last month (before the Jaipur incident) to ask me to be chief guest at his Rotary Club function. I had persistently refused such invitations in the past and my immediate response was a straight no. Then he went on to say that he had put up 40 lakhs for Shatranj and urged me to accept the invitation if only for the sake of his association with the film. Although wholly against my principle, I accepted for your sake and for the sake of the film. Dossani came again the other day to hand over the invitation which has my name on it. I should warn you that I will not hesitate for a moment to let him down regardless of consequences unless the situation in Calcutta improves within the next few days.

You can talk to Sunil about it and make what arrangements you can, but do treat this as most urgent. Since this directly affects my work, perhaps you can give me some idea of the financial situation at present, so that I may know where we and the film stand.

Yours,

Manik-da

~

In the end, even after repaying all the debts I had accrued to finance the film and after paying everyone off, my so-called friends still went to Manik-da (as seen in the above letter), telling him that I had not cleared my debts. They complained to him that I had interfered with their work and had shown inflated expenditures. Earlier, in my naivety, I had thought that people who are doing noble work automatically turn into noble people. How wrong I was!

Once things had relatively settled down and my relationship with Manik-da had resumed its previous warmth, I was reminded once again what a great teacher he was. He, too, had had to bear his share of personal criticism and slander. A professor at the Film and Television Institute of India, a small-time Bengali producer, government sycophants, journalists and even old friends had turned against him at various times. But he would always say, 'Suresh, often the best thing is not to respond to personal criticism or the matter blows up.'

He was blamed for everything, from destroying the other well-known Bengali film-maker Ritwik Ghatak, who later became the head of the FTII, to not being critical enough of the government (through his films), and even for being the 'peddler of India's poverty', as many of his films depicted the poor and marginalized people of Bengal. But he refused to comment on any of this. So, when I was finally able to explain things to him, he understood and, with a smile, offered the usual advice: 'Best not to respond.'

8

Post-production

After the shooting wrapped up, we went into post-production, which entailed hard work for all of us. As always, Manik-da did the editing and the spotting (the subtitles), but we also had to work on foreign translations, contact film festivals, set up distributors and deal with the government and its censorship, regulations and mountains of paperwork.

Film censorship in India among the most stringent in the world. The government kept, and continues to keep, a tight grip on absolutely everything in the country. India, at that time, followed a socialist model of government, which meant it had all the bureaucratic control of a Soviet regime without the Gulags and the terror. Thus, the governance was sardonically dubbed the 'licence permit raj'. This meant that whether you wanted to start an industry or undertake any kind of business activity, from commerce to cinema, various licences and permits had to be required.

Even today, each film is checked by a government-appointed censor board before public exhibition. Prior to a film's submission, a script must be written for the board, containing all the shots, scenes and dialogues as they appear in the final version. This script is generally written by specialists in the field (usually assistant directors or assistant editors) hired by the producer. This 'censor script' and the actual film are then submitted to the board. If it objects to any portions, these must be cut. If approved, it issues a certificate that has to be attached to the first reel of the film before it can be publicly shown. Not surprisingly, this can cause unforeseen delays and involves extra work.

A licence was needed to buy raw stock, for all foreign sales agreements, to export a film, even to send a film to foreign film festivals. With absolutely everything requiring a government licence or permission, schedules were upset, overseas agreements and release dates were thrown into turmoil. No commitments could be made because you never knew *if* and *when* a licence would be given. This is what Ray refers to in one of his letters as 'bureaucratic shilly-shallying'.

7/7/77

Dear Suresh,

Herewith the amended credit list.

As you can see, the acknowledgement list is an endless one—but obligatory. I have decided to put it at the end of the film as a rolling title superimposed over a freeze of the last shot. In the brochure it can go as it is at the bottom of the list.

Problem: Sunil is not happy with the 'production manager' credit. In any case, Bhanu[1] is the production manager, and he would not want to share it with anybody else (rightly, I think). Perhaps you can come up with a special credit for Sunil. He feels he should be credited as 'assistant producer', but this is something you should work out with Sunil. Javed, I had always thought of as the 'dialogue assistant', and not as assistant director. Since this gives him a solo credit, he shouldn't complain. I think the name of Mr Bels[2] should be included in the list of actors, but I don't know the first name. Uma[3] does. And what about the twenty-four officers from Delhi?

I had said that I would come to Bombay to OK

---

1. Bhanu Ghosh.

2. Mr Bels, a foreign diplomat cast as a British officer in the marching scene.

3. Uma da Cunha, liaison officer and publicist.

Rammohan's drawings for the animation, but I find he's so tied up with the editing and the music that I suggest as an alternative that Rammohan should send his detailed storyboard to me in Calcutta. This I could then approve or amend and send back. Can you talk to Rammohan and convey this to him? I shall need the finished thing by 20 in order to be able to compose and record the music by 25. We have booked HMV on 23/24/25 for the recording.

Babu,[4] Nemai[5] and Sumantra[6] are producing the stills. Sunil will be able to send them to you tomorrow. I'm also arranging to send the costumes for Zehra; Shama has just sent me the list. I'm preparing a few roughs for ads for Zehra and will send them on as soon as ready.

Best,

Yours,

Manik-da

28 July 1977

Dear Suresh,

Sunil has given me your letter. There has never been any question of your 'bending' for my sake, as there is none now. You must recall that in the early stages I supported

---

4. Sandip Ray's pet name.

5. Nemai Ghosh, stills photographer.

6. Sumantra Ghosal, son of the Ghosals, now a well-known ad film-maker.

you against Bansi when I felt he was making exorbitant demands (although I realize now that he hasn't gone over budget, and you too must have realized that the sets are going to add enormously to the attraction of the film). Where I was hurt was in your attitude towards the crew. Any insult to them, direct or indirect, I regard as an insult to myself. It is possible that your definition of an insult is not the same as mine, and perhaps we should have had a clear discussion on this aspect before we started shooting. I am proud of my crew because I feel Ashok, Bhanu, Purnendu, Pocha, Bolai, Trailokya, etc. are truly dedicated workers who are willing to give their all for the good of the film. Some of them may have their little foibles—but who doesn't?—and who cares if such shortcomings are offset by their skill in their particular jobs? Without my being there, they would all have quit. In the 25 years I've been in this line, I've never faced a situation like this. Can you wonder that I should lose my equanimity? Since you talk of bending, can you cite an instance where you had to do so? Have I ever asked for anything more than was required for the good of the film? I thought we had agreed on what was good for *Shatranj* even before we started shooting. And you had the advantage of a fully prepared script where, as producer, you didn't run the risk of the director springing unpleasant surprises on you. How can the question of bending arise unless I make unreasonable demands? I must make it clear, though, that I do not think it unreasonable to expect decent treatment of my crew on location.

However, let me report on the work in Lucknow and

Bombay. We finished dubbing Hari[7] and Amjad, and also
the retakes of Farida, Farrookh [sic] and Leela Mishra.
The Lucknow shots were also all taken. There are three
shots (one day's work) still to be taken in Calcutta: 1)
Nawab watching pigeons 2) Dismounting of guns (in Fort
William) and 3) Sacks of mohurs passing from Awadh
coffer to EI Co coffer. Amitabh[8] being away in Kashmir, I
have left instructions with Shama and Javed to supervise the
recording of the narration in my absence. I had expected
to bring back the dialogue tracks of the Attenborough
scenes, but Narinder has apparently been too busy to
transfer these. I must tell you that this is going to hold up
our editing since we have already edited everything else.

---

7. Sanjeev Kumar's nickname.

8. Amitabh Bachchan narrated the film's animation sequence
that depicted the relationship between the East India Company
and the nawabs of Awadh. Ray had told me he was keen to
have Amitabh do the narration, so I requested Tinnu to ask the
superstar. Amitabh and he had been friends since K.A. Abbas's
Saat Hindustani, Amitabh's first film. When Amitabh graciously
agreed to narrate the sequence, I became anxious since I thought
he might ask for an exorbitant amount, which would make a dent
on our already stretched budget. But Amitabh told Tinnu that if I
ever mentioned paying him again, he would not do the work. I was
enormously relieved but wanted to give the actor a gift as a token
of my deep appreciation. Once the recordings were done, Tinnu
suggested the perfect gift: the latest Kodak projector with a built-in
pull-out screen. Amitabh was fond of making Super-8mm films.
When I sent it to him, he wrote me this thank you note: 'Thanks
for the marvellous gift! You're not getting it back even if Manik-da
rejects the commentary. Wishing the "Chess Players" all success.'

Narinder must give us top priority or I can't guarantee that I'll finish the final cut by the end of July. Narinder has suggested that we do the channelling also in Bombay so that he may be available for occasional transfer jobs. I think this is a suitable suggestion. Accordingly, I have asked Tinnu to book an editing room for us from Aug 4 for 10 days. We have already booked Rajkamal for mixing for 4 days from Aug 16. For channelling and mixing, I'll have to have with me Prilal, Kashi, Prince, Babu and one production man (Bhanu or Anil). I've told Uma to book us at the Shalimar. Monku will stay with her friends the Imams.

Rammohan wants me in Bombay for a day or two after he's finished the drawings for the animations. He wants my OK before he actually exposes them. I reckon this would be about a fortnight from now.

Best,

Yours,

Manik-da

27/7/77

Dear Suresh,

I suggest pushing back the release by at least a fortnight. Here's a simple calculation to show why 16 would be cutting it too fine:

RR finishes on 19

Rajkamal will take at least ten days to develop the sound—21

Sound and picture sent to Madras on 22—received 23—(this is being optimistic)

Negative cutting will take a minimum of five days—29

Soumendu will take a minimum of ten days—7 September already

Then censorship, etc.

I think it would be most unwise to rush things at this stage. Postponement would help both Zehra and Sud at HMV,[9] who wants to bring out the first recording to coincide with the opening. Besides, there are a few things to do in Bombay apart from just channelling and RR—Shabana and Hari have a few lines of dubbing, Amjad has to record the song and Amitabh has to re-record a few lines of the commentary.

Also, I shall need a ½ shift in a recording studio to record two pieces of music for which no hands were available in Calcutta. We can still keep comfortably to our RR dates though.

I've been expecting a phone call from you re: my trip to Delhi.

Best,

Manik-da

Dear Suresh,

Within ½ an hour of speaking to you on the phone this morning, I received a copy of the latest (Autumn) *Sight & Sound* by air. There is a full-page ad for the London Film

9. Anil Sud, CEO of His Master's Voice (HMV).

Festival with a still from *Shatranj* featured prominently. It would appear that they have already printed the programme and I don't see how you can get out of it now without considerable embarrassment. I should make every effort to straighten out the difficulties and keep our commitment. Favourable reviews in London at this stage would also make things easier for you at this end—now that you are left largely to fend for yourself. I know the situation is very complex—most of the complexity arising out of Dossani backing out—nevertheless a very great effort and an exploration of all possible avenues seem to be indicated in order to avoid an all-round disaster. All of this is a great pity, and it seems it's going to take a lot of zest out of my holiday trip. However, I do hope some miracle will happen and everything will come out right at the end. Do keep me posted.

My Manali address will be:

[address deleted to preserve privacy]

Best,

Manik-da

6/10/77

Dear Suresh,

Herewith 12 reels of spotting sheets. Reels 12 and 14 will be ready tomorrow morning. I'll ask Sunil to send it by hand of some messenger so that no time is lost.

As you can see, a lot of work has gone into the

translation. I'm afraid you did a very rush job.[10] It's still not 100 % satisfactory, but this is the best that could be done in the time that we had. I also discovered that the censor script has a lot of mistakes and omissions in it.

The snag is that this is the only copy. Perhaps you could get hold of a typist here to make some copies for you—one to be sent to me in Calcutta. And what about the French translation? Who does it and where and when? It hardly seems likely that we can get a subtitled copy ready in time for the Paris screening. However, do what is possible under the circumstances.

I hope you've regained your voice by now. We leave for Kulu-Manali on 11 and will be back in Calcutta on 25 latest.

I'm taking FUJI Print No. 1 with me for screening at Society[11] on 9 morning. After that the print will be free.

Manik-da

~

For the negative of the film we used Eastman Kodak raw stock, considered to be the best in the world. At that time, due to the weak condition of the Indian economy and its foreign exchange reserve, mostly ORWO raw stock (both positive and negative) was being imported from East Germany. Since our trade and economy were aligned more with the Soviet Union, we could pay for all

---

10. Does not refer to me but rather to those ones who prepared the censor script.

11. A cinema hall in Calcutta.

our imports from the Soviet bloc in Indian rupees rather than hard currency such as dollars or pounds sterling. Of the three raw stocks available back then—Kodak, ORWO and Fuji—ORWO was the cheapest and the least preferred. But since Kodak and Fuji were only allowed into the country with import licences issued against the export of completed films, they usually had to be bought from private film distributors and exporters by paying a huge black market premium.

Prints of our film for important release centres and film festivals were made on Fujicolor, but since this was financially prohibitive for all prints, we often had to use ORWO for less important release centres.

8/10/77

Dear Suresh,

Herewith the 2 remaining reels. I had left the other 12 reels with Soumendu with instructions to hand them over to you as soon as you arrived, but I learnt later that you had postponed your Madras trip and asked for the spotting sheets to be sent to you in Bombay. I believe this was done immediately.

I can see that bureaucratic shilly-shallying[12] has upset our whole programme. This is not the first time that such

12. A reference to sending *Shatranj Ke Khilari* to the London Film Festival, for which government permission was required.

a thing has happened though. As far as I can see, only the London festival screening is now a certainty. I doubt if we can make it to Paris. What about the French translation and the French subtitling?

Since I can't cut short my trip to Manali, why don't you have your Bangalore opening on 21 anyway? Is my presence absolutely essential? Think about it.

Best,

Yours,

Manik-da

27/10/77

My dear Suresh,

I doubt if I can come to Bombay for the screening on 30—the Manali trip was quite hectic—but I'd like to request you to invite the following to the screening:

1. Mr Subhas Ghosal
2. Mr and Mrs Imam

I do hope you will see a good print. Ideal would be Fuji No. 3—if you have access to it.

I had a call from the London Film Festival yesterday. They are, naturally, desperately keen to show the film— but I couldn't give them much hope. Do keep on trying, however, and keep me posted.

I hope you realize how anxious I am about the fate of the film.

Best,

Yours,

Manik-da

Nov 2, '77

My dear Manik-da,

It is not in my nature to wallow in self-pity. When ideas I cherish, or things I have helped built, crumble in front of me because of underhanded attacks by elements that one has implicitly trusted, my immediate reaction is to get up and hit right back. It is further not in my nature to call upon higher powers to defend me until and unless the fight has totally exhausted me. I do not call upon elephant guns to defend me in a fight that can be won by a hand-to-hand combat.

It is not only the established mafia who are against *Shatranj*; there is also a section of the artsy-craftsy, culture-vulture crowd who consider themselves to be the arbitrators of taste in cinema. But in front of *Shatranj*, to use Mao's phrase, they are paper tigers. We will definitely win.

I am enclosing copies of some letters that I hope will constitute enough proof that I am not against *Shatranj* going to London or other festivals.[13] A certain doubt has been created by some people who have in the past (and now) accused me of 'paranoia' and 'masochism'. Considering the enormous stresses I am under, I am glad to observe that the state of my mental health is sound.

---

13. People were once again trying to create a rift between Manik-da and me by insinuating that I was against sending my own film to the London Film Festival.

None of my neuroses are self-destructive. I guess neuroses are like germs—some benevolent and some malignant.

We will win.

Suresh

Enclosures:

1. Letter to Gemini dated 29 October
2. Letter to director of film festival dated 25 October
3. Letter to Sapphire Movies dated 21 September
4. Letter from Sapphire Movies dated 3 October

> This letter is sufficient reason why the established mafia have to be fought tooth and nail—and why the fight has to be won.
>
> A big handicap I face is insufficient experience in 'street fighting' (I have been taught to 'play cricket' in polite drawing room conversations), but I am learning, and learning fast.

5. Letter to Uma dated 2 November

> Reaction to Shatranj by all who have seen it is absolutely super. One ardent fan from the established cinema that you have won is Prakash Mehra[14] (*Zanjeer, Hera Pheri, Khoon Pasina*). He has expressed a desire to distribute it in Delhi-Uttar Pradesh. Also Amitabh and Vinod Khanna[15]

---

14. The producer–director who made Amitabh Bachchan an all-time superstar with his film *Zanjeer*. He did finally distribute *Shatranj Ke Khilari* in the Delhi–UP territory.

15. Vinod Khanna, a superstar in his time, who briefly rivalled Amitabh Bachchan's popularity.

have been raving about it all over town. Things are definitely looking up. Our own cast are walking tall with all the kudos their performances are getting. The intuitive faith I had expressed, vide my letter to you, on reading the first draft of the screenplay has come true. It is a great film.

Best,
Suresh

3/11/77

Dear Suresh,

Your fat envelope was most welcome. I have a very clear picture of the situation now. Is N.N. Sippy[16] the producer–distributor who is connected with Hrishikesh Mukherji [sic]?[17] If so, then I shouldn't be surprised if Hrishi turns out to have a hand in the machinations. Remember how eager he was to throw a spanner into the works in the early stages of the production? However, I do hope things will straighten out in the near future. But one must fend against over-optimism. *Shatranj* is a film for a specialized audience, as even the screenplay must have suggested. I believe this audience is yet to be tapped, and I also believe that it is large enough to make such a

16. A prominent producer and distributor of Hindi cinema. He bought the film for the Bombay territory and subsequently refused to release it.

17. Hrishikesh Mukherjee, a famous Hindi film director.

film a viable proposition. Incidentally, Charles Cooper of Contemporary[18] has suddenly come into the picture, offering to advance money against the film in case we are short of funds. Personally I feel that Connoisseur[19] are better distributors and Pallanca a more honest man than Cooper.[20] I want you to keep this in mind when the time comes to negotiate a deal.

The enclosed clipping would be of interest to you. I assume this is the story given out by our friend Kumar.[21] I've had to answer a barrage of telephone calls arising out of this, and will probably have to continue doing so over the next few weeks!

The letter, cables and phone calls I've received from Bombay in the last few days have been most heartening. Have any of the critics seen the film? Bikram?[22] Dharker?[23]

Yours,

Manik-da

---

18. Contemporary Films, a prominent distributor of art films in the UK.

19. Connoisseur Films, also a prominent distributor of art films. They distributed our film in the UK.

20. Distributors in Ireland and the UK.

21. Dhananjaya Kumar, the distributor in the US.

22. Bikram Singh, the doyen of film critics in India.

23. Anil Dharker, a prominent film critic.

8/11/77

Dear Suresh,

Herewith the modified version of the spotting sheet. Where a title is to be split up into two, I have indicated the split by an oblique line and also indicated the new footage. There should be no difficulty now.

I wonder if anyone noticed at the screening that Agha's[24] name has been dropped inadvertently. I don't suppose there's anything one can do about it now.

A long cable from Berlin[25] requesting us to withdraw the film from London, Paris, Chicago and Rotterdam so that Berlin can have it in the competitive section.

Best,
Yours,
Manik-da

Nov. 14, '77

My dear Manik-da,

Thank you for your letter. I am now in Delhi and will be leaving for Bombay in two days' time. I have come

---

24. He played the son of the dying lawyer from whom the chess players borrow a chess set.

25. Berlin, Cannes and Venice are the three top competitive film festivals and only accept those films that have not yet been shown at any other festival in the world. The film was originally shown at the London Film Festival; despite that, Berlin wanted and accepted it in the competitive section.

here for a final settlement of the matter.[26] In case this negotiation fails, I will have no choice but to take the matter before the Producers' Council and the High Court. I was trying to avoid this step and was seeking a more amicable settlement.

I feel very encouraged by the response to the show I had in Bombay. There was a fair spectrum of people. I purposely kept the critics out, as I felt it would not be a good idea to get the reviews until a date for the release is fixed. Only Anil Dharker came, with the understanding that he will not review the film just yet. According to his reaction, he was rendered 'speechless'.

Ismail Merchant also came, and he's become the biggest propagandist for the film. He was recently in Delhi and was raving about the film to mutual friends. My belief that it will shatter the stupor our audiences have been subjected to has become firmer. However, Shatranj will definitely be instrumental in changing the psyche of film-makers in this country for years to come.[27] Even though I have no mechanical and graphic data to go by, I feel 100 % sure that it will be a 'safe' proposition. In the absence of firm data, one can only project one's intuition and make it reach that nebulous area of the future and come up with an answer to one's uncertainties. My intuition says yes! It will be a film that will have far-ranging effects on

---

26. That the first distributors had all backed out, saying the film was not commercially viable.

27. Wishful thinking on my part that an arthouse film would be a mainstream hit, and then mainstream backers might back arthouse cinema.

the future course of Hindi cinema. And something that has a chance (even though a small one) of changing the consciousness of time is worth fighting for.

I whip myself into a high state of optimism because it's necessary to keep the adrenalin flowing. The flow of adrenalin is very necessary if I am to save myself from falling into a paralytic depression. The one grave consequence of *Shatranj*'s failure would be to force me into making 'formula cinema', and that is one consequence I absolutely refuse to acknowledge until everything possible has been done. I don't suppose it will matter a great deal to people in the industry, since then I will have fit their image of me anyway—that of a conventional producer, out to make a fast buck and nothing else. But it will drive me to a state of callousness and cynicism. It's still a long way until there, and I might as well try my best until then. It is too important a battle for me to lay down arms and hold my head in my hands and weep in helplessness.

N.N. Sippy is not Hrishikesh's producer. That is N.C. Sippy. In fact, N.C. Sippy is interested in buying the film for Bombay after he sees it. I will show it to him as soon as I get to Bombay. He's Amitabh's partner in distribution and I suppose Amit plugged in for us. He and Jaya were very impressed by the film.

I think I will deal with Pallanca rather than with C. Cooper. Most people seem to have a negative view of Charles Cooper. That would have been an important bonus of going to London. Our sale could have materialized.

With warm regards to you and your family,

Yours,

Suresh

Suresh,

Re: Awards—the convention should be followed. In other words, cash award for best film should go to the producer. In the national awards, the director gets a cash prize for the best film too—in addition to the cash he gets if he is nominated the best director. In international fests, too, if the picture gets a prize, it goes to the producer. There are other special awards for the directors.

[unsigned, but handwritten by Ray]

~

With all the problems revealed in these letters, it is obvious that *Shatranj Ke Khilari* was off to a rough start in terms of release and general acceptance. Of course, as with all Ray films, arthouse cinema worldwide was enthralled by the concept of a non-Bengali Ray film and was anxious to view it, but Hindi cinema still ruled India and our film did not remotely fit into its accepted formula.

9

The Release and After

♟♟♟♟♟♟

In India, there are six designated territories for the distribution of movies: Five are domestic and the sixth covers the overseas market. While Hollywood has territories divided by language, all with a ratio of worth, the five Indian territories are approximately equally priced. Each one has many distribution companies. The best deal for producers is minimum guarantee (MG), which is a non-refundable amount the distributor gives up front, whether the film is a hit or a flop. The next best option is a sharing agreement in which the distributor invests in publicity and the film prints, and then all accrued profits are shared in a pre-agreed ratio. The least desirable is an advance. It is actually a loan in which the distributor has to repay whatever difference is not recouped.

Shatranj Ke Khilari had made headlines across India when it was first announced in 1975, excitedly hailing 'Ray's First Film in Hindi!' As such, I had no problems selling it to distributors from all five territories; Ray's name was a big draw. However, after viewing the film, they decided that since it was an art film it would not make money and all five backed out. Eventually, I found other distributors and we released the film all over India, but the damage had already been done, both in terms of delay and saleability. Film, like fruit, goes past its 'best by' date quickly if it doesn't hit the market right away. The six to seven months lost in this process affected the film's commercial success. We had to stagger the release across India, instead of releasing it simultaneously, as it should have. Manik-da had wanted—and hoped—that the film would be shown in cinemas nationwide, but that was not to be. As word got out that the original distributors thought the film would flop financially, we were unable to get good distribution packages. Overseas sales became the only hope of recouping my investment. Over the next five to six years, foreign distribution slowly made up the money lost in India, but that's a long time for debts and interest to accrue.

Most critics in India gave the film good reviews, preventing it from being a complete box-office disaster, but not enough to recover the investment. International response was generally very positive.

28/1/78

Dear Suresh,

I was delighted to know that the LKO[1] screening went well. I do hope this augurs well for the film, and I do hope that the exemption will be granted[2]—at least in UP. I found a tremendous interest in the film in Benaras—which is unique in having a Bengali population of 1,50,000 who all follow Urdu. I still feel that the picture should open in one theatre in the big cities rather than in a chain. Although I don't doubt that a lot of people are going to like the film, from our side we should create the impression that this is a special kind of a movie.

As for para-dubbing, I'm not yet sure what exactly you're planning. I hope the original version will play in the principal towns (at least in the main theatres). The actual work of para-dubbing—of which I'm no expert—may have to be done without my presence; the reason being my very tight schedule over the next 3/4 months. Here it is:

Feb 1–5: Rotterdam
Feb 7–25: shooting in Benaras
Feb 28–March 6: Berlin
March 10–20: shooting in Calcutta
April 1: depart for USA

---

1. Abbreviation for Lucknow, the capital of Uttar Pradesh.

2. Exemption from entertainment tax on film tickets.

As for the 24 Feb opening (Delhi & LKO?), I may finish shooting a day or two earlier and make it. If not, I shall try to come down just for the opening provided suitable flights or trains are available. As for USA and our friend Kumar, I find it hard to explain to him why a long stay is out of the question; but I will tell you—every other day I have to take a pill (Lasix) for my hypertension; this means I have to stay at home for an 8-hour stretch in order to get the salt out of my system. When I'm shooting, my pressure keeps down (this applies to any kind of work—physical or mental—which I enjoy and which stimulates me). But on hectic foreign trips, especially of the kind that Kumar is planning, my pressure keeps mounting till I'm back home and in a position to resume medication. Kumar must somehow be made to realize this. The trouble seems to be the dates in Washington and LA. Washington has fixed the showing on 2, while Filmex starts on 13. Frankly I feel it is more important to keep the Washington date than the LA. I don't think Filmex has acquired much prestige yet, even in the USA. In the past all my films have opened in the USA without my presence. I realize that Shatranj is a special case and that is why I've agreed to come. But Kumar mustn't insist on a fortnight's stay. I hope you'll try and make him see reason.

Yours,
Manik-da

Jan 30, '78

My dear Manik-da,

Regarding the UK distribution: the prices offered by Cooper and Pallanca will not be acceptable to the government.[3] The problem we face there is neither one has a good idea of what the 'immigrant' audience attendances are like in the UK. To give an example: For *Rajnigandha* I had got £16,000 outright, whereas Cooper is offering only $10,000 outright. This he has subsequently changed to a sharing offer. As another example: Even a tiny spot like Mozambique has given us the equivalent of Rs 24,000 through IMPEC.[4] And Tunisia is offering Rs 37,500. In view of this, both the Cooper and Pallanca offers are too little. And this can't be discussed via letters, so I am waiting to see them when I go to London. The release in India and its result will give us a fair idea of immigrants' response to the film in the UK. And mostly the immigrants are from the Hindi and Urdu (Pakistan) speaking areas of the subcontinent and Africa. And added to this are the views of both Robinson & Gibbs[5] that *Shatranj* could go for a general release in the UK.

Release dates of Delhi–UP: 24 Feb. That means the Delhi première will be on 23 night. I think UP releases are

---

3. The government had to approve all export contracts to ensure they were not being undervalued and the difference stashed abroad.

4. Indian Motion Pictures Export Corporation, one of the ubiquitous government bodies controlling Indian films.

5. David Robinson and Patrick Gibbs, British film critics.

a day earlier, which means the LKO première will be on 22 night. Will it be possible for you to finish your shooting before then? It will be of great importance for you to attend, and I would also like the crew to come with you.

Regarding Bombay & Eastern Circuit: Interestingly, there is complete silence from the trade—no enquiries even. This is what I call circumstantial evidence of some quarters wanting to hold the film. Even a film like *Rajnigandha* used to get enquiries, so do all films even if they are bad. But in our case—complete silence—I am not discouraged, as I feel we will make our point after the LKO screening, where I told you we had a totally uncontrolled audience of 800 people. I feel very confident that Shatranj will make the breakthrough we are hoping for. No! At no point have I imagined that it will do a business of two to three times its cost. My confidence lies only as far as my belief that it will easily pay for itself, along with the distributors' commission. But once it breaks that barrier, then anything can happen. Haryana[6] has asked us for a screening in Chandigarh on 11 Feb.

Release of the music record: I will be requesting HMV to release the record in Delhi-UP by the 7 February. I hope the timing is correct in relation to the release date. Thereafter, they can release it elsewhere in India and also overseas.

Further, may I please ask HMV to go ahead with the dialogue record? I assume they have already taken your view on it. In any case, I will ask them to meet you before you leave for Benaras.

---

6. The screening was to be exempted from entertainment tax in the state.

I feel sure that the movement you started with *Pather Panchali* will come into full swing, and stay, over the next two years, if not earlier. The 'commercial' cinema, I think, has got itself into a hopeless mess by announcing so many multi-star-cast films. The hottest (box office) film in Delhi and Bombay is Rajshri's *Dulhan Wahi Jo Piya Man Bhaye*. It has all new stars, and has been released without a single hoarding or poster. And it's creating havoc. The new girl Rameshwari is very good. I think all this augurs well for Indian cinema today. When this happens, then what we can make is wide open. To break the possibilities wide open has been my endeavour as a producer. And I hope it will continue to be so.

Regards,
Suresh

May 29, '78

My dear Manik-da,

I've been wanting to come to Calcutta but I can't afford to at this time. I am using all available funds to pay off personal loans of friends and relatives, so I feel guilty in spending money on air fares, and I can't bear long journeys by trains—especially in this hot weather.

I wanted to discuss two things with you:

1. The possibility of editing down two scenes in *Shatranj*: (a) Outram and Fayrer (b) Amjad's long monologue. Both these scenes are a bit too long

and make the audience restless in an otherwise very absorbing film. It is not absolutely essential to do this if you feel it will detract from the film. Only in the case of the Fayrer scene can we avoid having two separate versions if the scene can be reduced to near half its length.

2. I have already talked to Shyam Benegal[7] about doing a film with him around Oct/Nov. If everything is all right with you, and no great bitterness remains with your unit about the *Shatranj* experience, I would very much like to do a film with you again. I guess because of your previous commitments, you will not be free before March '79, which suits me fine. I would like to make the announcement concurrently with Shyam's film, and we could work out the details later. I personally would like to do a co-production in English with an international cast, but the choice is up to you in this matter.[8]

I am still confident that the film will make a strong showing at the Bombay and Calcutta releases. The Delhi–UP release got badly bungled in that too many stations were covered simultaneously. For Calcutta we're thinking of a single-print release. By August, we will also have our English subtitled print back[9] and we can release that in Calcutta.

---

7. A prominent film director and leading figure of the art cinema movement in India.

8. I went on to make *Gandhi*.

9. The original went missing.

After the release of the last production and before the beginning of the next one, I always get acutely depressed. The best remedy for me in such a state is to go into complete solitude; catch up on my reading and let my thoughts wander; dream about the future and sort out the past.

Do please write to me; and if the situation changes I will try to come to Calcutta before you leave for London.

I hope boudi's thumb gets better soon.

Yours,

Suresh

1/6/78

My dear Suresh,

Pablo[10] dropped in this morning and gave me your letter. I agree with you that the film would improve, pace-wise, if the 2 scenes you mention were shortened. With the Outram–Fayrer scene this shouldn't be a problem and I know exactly where the cut should come. With the Amjad scene, I'll have to sit with a print and work out a possible way. It's not as easy, because there are very careful and logical transitions from mood to mood leading to one of defiance. You may recall that it was because I realized that it wasn't possible to justify Wajid without a great deal of verbalization that at one point I decided to

10. Pablo Bartholomew, now a famous photojournalist. *Shatranj Ke Khilari* was his first film job.

drop the project. I persisted largely because you seemed so crestfallen when I told [you]. Perhaps I also persuaded myself that Amjad's performance would hold the scene together. I now realize, as I've often done before, that it doesn't pay to mistrust one's instincts. However, whatever cuts are to be made will have to be made by me, and for that I shall need a print. Or would you rather have me come down to Bombay? I could do that in mid-June—stop over for a day on my way to London—if that's not too late for you.

Now for your second proposal. While I can assure you that there is no feeling of bitterness left in me, I'm not sure if it would be wise to think of renewing a working relationship just yet. At any rate, I can't speak for the rest of my crew. I have lost, at least temporarily, my zest for making Hindi films. The proposals which I have already been asked to consider are: (a) A documentary on Rajasthani music for French TV, which I have accepted and which will keep me occupied for the rest of the year; (b) A 3-part film for BBC (each 90 minutes long) on any subject or subjects of my own choice. Were I to accept this, it would keep me wholly tied up right through '79 & part of '80. (c) A proposal from UNO to make a film on the 'horrors & miseries of war', for worldwide TV screening. This one has only just come. (d) A revival of *The Alien* under a major US company backing with an updated script and a new title. This must be made soon, if at all. I'm waiting to find out whether we are free to go ahead without reference to Mike Wilson, who was originally setting it up, and Columbia—the original sponsors. In addition to all these, there are two Bengali subjects which I want to do very much. Just now I'm too full of the new film to think clearly ahead, but I see no way how you can announce my name along with Shyam's. I hope you'll appreciate my difficulty.

Yours,
Manik-da

July 27, '78

My dear Manik-da,

I hope everything is going well with your new film.

The print of *Shatranj* was sent to Calcutta sometime back and I hope you've had a chance to edit it. I have no news from the lab regarding this, so please let me know.

The BBC contract was filed for registering 3 weeks back. You may have read in *Screen*[11] that the JCCI and E[12] are taking unduly long to register the overseas contract. They are still processing applications of 18th June 1978, whereas ours is of 10th July or so. It's very infuriating and I'm breathing down their backs.

Mr Pallanca, who is doing the theatrical release, has been sent the spot sheets by me. To avoid confusion (like in America) I have sent him a photostat of your original.

The film is not faring well in Bangalore. We have

---

11. A major film weekly of India.

12. Joint Chief Controller of Imports and Exports: During our 'socialist' days we had to register all import/export contracts with this body.

released the original English version. I can't figure out why.

There was again some confusion over the Cambridge festival. Pam telephoned Murthy at FFC[13] to get in touch with me. I explained that I had already spoken to Carol Holsan when I was in London. I don't know why the confusion occurred again.

The Indian High Commission in Australia has practically blown our sale by having a publicly announced show—this despite their telling me through FFC & the Directorate of Film Festivals that it will be an 'Invitees Only' show. I guess the spell of bad luck is still dogging me and it's infuriating to be so helpless and not be able to do something about it.

As it is I've made enough enemies. Taking on the external affairs and I&B ministries will be a self-destructive exercise. God knows, I feel like doing it to prick some needles in their callousness. Maybe like most others, I should join the bastards—a terrifying prospect.

I'm in a quandary: *Shatranj* has wiped out my total liquidity and the recovery depends on overseas sales. So far they are slow but my agent in NY is encouraging. I am considering going back to the university for two reasons: to be able to dispel my ignorance and put all the experiences in a proper prospective, and the student life will be cheap. Also I need to rebuild my optimism and drive for an ideal cinema. It's on the verge of crumbling like a sugar cookie. I'm just barely able to hold on. But

13. N.V.K. Murthy, general manager of the Film Finance Corporation, a government body responsible for financing 'art' cinema.

like I told you in London, at least I had fun, and I do not doubt the final value of *Shatranj* as a film.

Regards,
Suresh

24/10/78

Dear Suresh,

Many thanks for the cheque. You're right about the amount that you still owe me, but you can take your time over it.

I don't know if Sunil has informed you, but *Shatranj* is a great success in Calcutta and will very likely run till the end of the year. Word of mouth is very strong and lots of people are going back for a second and third look.

The Gemini people are crazy to turn out such bad prints. Nambi[14] was down here a couple of weeks ago and I gave him a piece of my mind, but they seem to be incorrigible. I must send them a strong note once again. Chakravarty, the distributor for our region, seems very upset that Sunil hasn't yet delivered the 5 or 6 prints that he was supposed to. Do you know anything about it, and can you make sure that this is done without delay?

The latest issue of *India Today* carries a cover story on Shyam in which Shashi[15] has a quote on *Shatranj*. Is he

---

14. Chief technician at Gemini Colour Laboratories.

15. Shashi Kapoor, actor–producer who produced a film that is set in the same period as *Shatranj Ke Khilari* called *Junoon* (1978), directed by Shyam Benegal.

out of his mind? I can't imagine a meaner statement from someone who is supposed to be among the more decent and intelligent of Bombay actors, and who is supposed to have stood up so far for serious, off-beat Hindi films.

We're coming to Bombay on Nov 4 for the re-recording of the new film and will stay (probably) at the Shalimar Hotel for about a fortnight. Could you inform Tinnu please? I hope to see you there.

Best,

Yours,

Manik-da

Oct 24th, '78

My dear Manik-da,

You must have received the copies of all my letters to Gemini, and must have also heard eyewitness reports on the prints. I just cannot tell you the trouble and agony caused by Gemini. They have consistently supplied us with bad prints.

Whatever the causes are, the fact seems to be that they just cannot/will not give us good prints. It will have an effect on them if you could write them a strong letter on the basis of evidence supplied by me.

One thinks that one's cap is full, that all the bad that has to happen has happened, but no! One still has to be ready for more, because it never seems to end. Can only hope one's inner core doesn't crack, that's all!

Warm regards,

Suresh

Oct 26th, '78

My dear Manik-da,

Thanks for your letter.

Sunil has already been keeping me informed on the film's progress in Calcutta, and I'm happy to hear it's faring well.

Regarding the prints, I've already given them[16] one more print, and another has been ordered at Gemini. Further prints can be supplied to them on payment, since the entire contract amount has not yet been received by me from the distributors. I think this matter is already being settled. From my side there is no problem.

I telephoned Gemini and they categorically told me that unless I pay they will not replace the print. Now this is a very surprising attitude, since I have paid them all their old bills. What is left to pay is for prints made afterwards, and there are some clarifications which they've not given me. Besides, it was settled that I will pay them on receiving the money from the BBC. It is obvious they agreed to this because they did supply us the prints for dispatch.

The new attitude is mere arm-twisting and blackmail, and their clutching at straws to get out of their responsibilities. The way future sales are affected is this: Yesterday I got a telex from my agent who is at Milan attending MIFED.[17] We have an Italian offer but they

_____

16. The Bengal distributors.

17. A well-known film and television festival.

want the negative to be sent to Rome for taking out prints. From the BBC experience they've lost all confidence in our quality. So I am in a quandary.

Still I hope they (Gemini) can see reason. Instead of acting tough they could try to give us the quality which they have in the past.

One always treads 'the razor's edge' between a heightened sensitivity and paranoia. I do not know what to believe; whether the rumours that somebody has been bribed at Gemini to harass us are correct or not. The Bombay prints were sent without the censor certificates, which could have resulted in a confiscation of the prints and the banning of the release. The BBC prints being rejected means that we probably can't play the film at the Academy[18] till next year (as per Mr Pallanca's letter to me). Whatever it is, the timing of both events has been such as to jeopardize us in a big way and delay the recovery of the investment. And to make buyers shy away from future purchases.

The only thing to do is wait and watch. Even 'hoping' seems to be meaningless.

I will be here when you come.

Regards,

Suresh

---

18. The cinema on Oxford Street where the film ended up running for nearly a year.

29/1/79

My dear Suresh,

Many thanks for the draft.

The Chess Players, as you probably know, has opened to superb reviews in London. I have received 3 clippings (*Guardian*, *Telegraph* and *Observer*), and all are first rate. A cable from Richard[19] suggests that this is the general tone of most of the reviews. I was wondering if Karanjia[20] could be persuaded to flash the news in *Screen* with suitable quotes. This may revive interest in the film at home, and also squash some of the rumours about lukewarm reception abroad.

New Delhi
Jan 31st, '79

My dear Manik-da,

Thanks for your letter. I was already in touch with Francis[21] to see if I could help in getting the clearances for the Rajasthan project;[22] I am sorry to hear that it is now to be postponed.

I am very happy to hear of the London reviews. If you

---

19. Richard Attenborough.

20. B.K. Karanjia, editor of *Screen* magazine, previously editor of *Fanfare* magazine.

21. Francis Wacziarg, a French businessman settled in India.

22. A documentary film project by Ray.

could send me the reviews, I am sure I could try to get a little write-up in Screen.

We've made sales to Iraq, Czechoslovakia, Poland and Switzerland (TV). Derek Hill is going to try to sell FRG[23] and Scandinavia for us. For France, one M. Lescure, who is the president of an association of 800 art cinemas in France, saw the film and will try to get us an outlet in France. If Germany and France go through, I will be financially in the black.

Only thing is that the 'traditional' overseas territories are not yet selling. Unfortunately, Kumar & Shankar[24] added to the scare by telling everybody the film is losing money in the USA. They've submitted me no accounts except saying the film has grossed 'over $1,00,000'. In that case, how they've lost I can't understand. Even in the past, we've exchanged letters in very strong language on this matter. This time they promised to bring details, but again the same vagueness and shilly-shallying, damaging the potential of the film.

They also have been giving the impression that they're very close to you, and are making a film with you. I don't understand what they're up to, particularly Kumar. I really don't care, except where they damage our interests, viz., Shatranj. Kumar may be shrewd (over-clever) business-wise but he's a naive and foolish professional. Even a fly-by-night person in our line is more professional than him.

It was only to build up the saleability of Shatranj that

23. Federal Republic of Germany.

24. The film's first distributors in the US and in Canada.

I wanted the statistics and also because it's my right since the film is on MG with them. Kumar doesn't understand this basic fact of life. He also seems to have the 'Krishna Shah delusion'—a peculiar characteristic of many Indians who settle abroad. The delusion being: We are white and all the Indians are bloody natives and the 'Great White Father' is going to take over because the 'Blackies' are so dumb. Kumar has surprises coming to him!

I'm mentioning the above to give you an example of how the problems come from unexpected quarters, and from people one implicitly trusts, who give the impression of being ardent supporters.

Junoon is doing average business. People are comparing it to *Shatranj* and are universally saying ours was a much better film. At least the audiences are discriminating enough to see that. Shyam has really taken a beating on the screenplay. But Shashi will not lose money. I don't think the film could have cost more than 25 lakhs, using *Shatranj* as a reference. And Shashi has already got 18 lakhs from overseas, which is more than what we have got so far. We will get more once the block of the traditional circuits are broken. That's where my anger with Kumar boils over. One is realistic enough to appreciate his hiding the returns from me, but to damage potential business, that's unforgivable.

If you would agree, I really want to make another film with you. I can arrange the money, since my credit is still good. Besides, I'm hopeful more overseas sales will go through and money will be coming by the time we get ready.

I'm more convinced than ever that your films are commercially viable, so I've no fear there. Now, of course, I know the game much better.

I'm not a person who settles for second best. If you do not make a film with me, I will go to Shyam as the next best man. But my heart is not in it.

Manik-da, if you are not committed to anything yet, please let's give it a go-together again. I know the 'commercial walas'[25] are scared—this time they'll really run. And believe me, they will buy our film.

I'm coming to Calcutta in the first week of Feb (around 7) on my way to Orissa. If you're there I'll definitely see you, and if we can work out something together it will give me the greatest thrill.

My warm regards to everybody. See you soon.

Yours,

Suresh

~

For the advertisement and publicity of the film we travelled to various cities of the world. Manik-da was fun to be with both at home and overseas. He had the curiosity of a child, making every activity an adventure. Like an obedient schoolboy, he would carry a shopping list from his family and friends for Harrods, London's famous department store, and would faithfully execute that duty first. Once that was done, he would get excited

25. Mainstream business people.

about going to a bookshop, music store or art supply store for himself. He looked forward to watching films and plays and visiting museums wherever we went, but not to social occasions, which he disliked with a passion. And yet, strangely enough, he seemed to have endless patience with the fools and social climbers he encountered when forced to attend these events, even though he saw right through them. Everywhere he went people instantly attached themselves to him in the hope of gaining profit simply from being seen with him.

I learnt a great deal from him during our travels—from film-making to lessons about every aspect of life and about living more consciously. Since he was a master of everything he attempted and a master of his emotions, just being around him was a constant learning experience. Sometimes the lessons were overt; at other times they were more subtle. When my blood would boil watching sycophants hover around him at public events, his patience would calm me.

Sometimes he taught me forcefully. On one occasion, I was all spruced up, ready to take the elevator at the Ashok Hotel in New Delhi, hoping to gain the attention of a gorgeous Sinhalese actress attending the same film festival we were, when the elevator door opened and there stood Manik-da.

'Baba, you are going to see *Andrei Rublev*?'

No I am not, Tall Man. I'm on a very different mission

tonight. And don't you try to bully me into going. Besides, who is Andrei Rublev anyway? Never heard of him.

'You have been seeing the Tarkovsky films, haven't you?'

No, I haven't. Don't know him either. Some Soviet-financed propaganda film-maker?

I stood sullenly in front of him, wishing this encounter had never happened.

'You must see it. It is one of the outstanding films of our times,' he said, looking deep into my eyes before he vanished.

Of course, I never did take the elevator. I hurried over to Plaza, where I sat sulking, chiding myself at having given into him yet again, when suddenly something changed. I felt myself being transported into a world of calm and incredible beauty. A film so gorgeous in visual imagery that I just sat in stunned silence, even during the intermission; a film that is a gift and will inspire me forever.

Great teachers teach you gently. It is only they who know if and when the student is ready for the lesson. Their love for their students makes them compassionate, ever watchful of digressions, like an indulgent mother.

~

I had heard that Manik-da had wanted to be a painter. During the promotional tour of the film, we were at the

Boston Museum of Fine Arts one day. The museum was closed to the public that day but was opened especially for us because it had sponsored our show. I can still picture him, standing thoughtfully before an exhibit, chewing on the plastic frame of his glasses, staring intently at a figure on an Inca fabric. I watched him silently for a few moments, wondering what was so engrossing. As if he could feel my gaze on him, he turned to me: 'Baba, see this? This is why I gave up painting. One cannot possibly improve upon this.'

I was taken aback. Neither my knowledge nor comprehension was deep enough to fathom this remark, until one day I understood. Perhaps he had felt that he could never produce a body of work that could compare with the masterpieces of the art world, but by choosing the medium of film, Manik-da definitely created far better cinema than what existed around him. And for this I salute him.

In our many travels together, we had only one ongoing disagreement: He was indifferent to food while I am a gourmand. Flavour, texture, aroma, presentation are very important to me—most likely a reaction to my student days abroad as a strict vegetarian in meat-eating countries, where for years all I could find to eat in restaurants was bread, baked potatoes or French fries with ketchup.

One day we were having lunch at a London restaurant. As I watched him chew on a leathery-looking sandwich—

which I would have immediately sent back—I felt deeply embarrassed at being his producer and providing him with such lousy fare. Not knowing what to do about the situation, I finally murmured:

'Manik-da, how is your sandwich?'

'It's okay.'

'Are you sure?' I asked, hoping he would say something objectionable about it so I could send it back and get him a better one.

'Yes. It's quite good, in fact!' he said much to my surprise.

Oh my God! He can't be real! I thought to myself. But he really meant it. His working lunch was always just a sandwich along with a piece of mithai, paan and endless cups of tea.

~

We were at the Berlin Film Festival in 1977 where *Shatranj Ke Khilari* was an official competition entry. When Steven Spielberg's *Close Encounters of the Third Kind*, the closing film of the festival, started playing I was thoroughly amused when one of the projectors failed. *So, it's not only us 'Third World' people who have glitches, even the efficient Germans fail sometimes!* After every reel the lights would come on in the auditorium while they manually inserted the next one. Finally, in the last reel the aliens came out of their spaceship. Manik-da and

I sat there stunned, until we finally dragged our eyes away from the screen and looked at one another in total disbelief. The beings looked *exactly* like Ray's description of them in the script and the sketches of his proposed film, *The Alien*, conceived long before in the 1960s.

The show ended and the lights came on.

'Did you see that, Baba?' Manik-da asked me with (for him) unusual agitation.

'Yes, Dada,' I replied sadly.

'Did you see how the alien looked? Do you remember my sketch of it?'

'Yes, I do, sir. It was exactly as you described and drew it in your script.' I could hardly bear to look in his eyes. 'I never would have thought that such a thing could happen in Hollywood; that they would actually stoop lower than our cut-throat Bombay film industry.'

The background to this travesty involves no less than David O. Selznick, one of Hollywood's greatest producers. Selznick had instituted a film award in Berlin named after himself, which Ray had won twice in a row. The first time he won, Selznick magnanimously asked him to come to Hollywood—this was a man who had discovered Fred Astaire, Ingrid Bergman, Alfred Hitchcock, among many others, and had produced such immortal films as *Gone with the Wind*, *King Kong*, etc.—but Ray did not respond. The second time he won, Selznick invited him to a private dinner in Berlin. 'Ray, why won't you come to Hollywood?' he inquired almost plaintively.

'Mr Selznick, I have heard of your famous memos[26] …
and I am sure I could never work that way,' Ray responded
with a wry smile. And that was the end of that. Selznick
never could lure him into his film realm, but Columbia
Studios finally did, and that is how the script of *The Alien*
got to be written. In the film studio's old manner of doing
things, they assigned Ray a producer, who unfortunately
fell out of favour with the studio bosses. The studio told
Ray that even though they wanted his film, they could not
do it with that particular producer. As luck would have
it, the producer, Mike Wilson, had registered the film in
both his and Ray's names, which made the studio shelve
the project. Meanwhile, the script went on to circulate in
Hollywood for years.

Back in the auditorium in Berlin, reeling from shock,
we were silent and remained so for the rest of the night.
What could we say? That in the face of Spielberg and
the awesome power of Hollywood we were mere 'Third
World' film-makers who were only allowed a total
allowance of 200 dollars a day for our business travels by
the bosses of our myopic socialist republic? Where would
we have the money or influence to fight this wrong?

Arthur C. Clarke, who wrote *2001: A Space Odyssey*
and was an admirer and friend of Ray, wrote a letter to

---

26. Selznick was a perfectionist and wanted total control over all
his films, sending endless memos to his directors, actors and crew
to get them to follow his wishes.

the *Times* newspaper in 1984, stating that when he had mentioned to Spielberg that he might be accused of plagiarism, Spielberg's reply had been a rather indignant: 'Tell Satyajit I was a kid in high school when his script was circulating in Hollywood!'

Much later, on one of my visits to Calcutta, while sitting in Manik-da's study, he opened a letter with a foreign stamp and postmark. He read the letter with unusual intensity, and then handed it to me. 'Read this,' he said, his voice flat.

I looked at the letter, my eyes immediately drawn to the letterhead, which read 'Swami Shiva Kalki'. The contents were intriguing, all about surrendering the rights to *The Alien*—the only film Ray had ever agreed to do in Hollywood. But what was even more intriguing was that the writer was a Buddhist monk in Sri Lanka!

'Remember *The Alien*, Baba?' Manik-da asked me, a suggestion of resignation on his face.

'Yes, sir. How could I ever forget?'

'Well, this is from the person who was to be the producer of the film. Now, apparently, Mike Wilson has become a Buddhist monk and lives in Sri Lanka ... and is concerned about his karma,' he added ruefully.

At times, it is true that life is stranger than fiction.

Besides the striking resemblance between the images of Ray's and Spielberg's aliens, what I remember most about the whole episode was Manik-da's verbal description of what he had written long before, which was identical to what was portrayed in the film: that the aliens were 'benign by nature, small and acceptable to children, possessed of certain supernatural powers, not physical strength but other kinds of powers, particular types of vision, and that they take interest in earthly things'.

In fact, this was not the only science fiction he had written. He had published a whole series in the genre. It was a subject of great fascination to him.

And to this very day, some models for extraterrestrials bear a close resemblance to Ray's sketches from the 1960s. So, the next time you see a picture, TV show or movie with a slim, silver-hued, shiny, wide-eyed alien, know that it arose from the ever-creative mind of one of the world's greatest film directors.

22/11/79

My dear Suresh,

The report in *India Today* is not strictly accurate. 'Mahakasher Doot'[27] was conceived as a short story, not

---

27. In *Mahakasher Doot*, Professor Shonku—a fictional Bengali scientist created by Satyajit Ray in a series of science-fiction books—tries to prove that mankind has prospered with the help of an alien civilization that comes to Earth every 5,000 years to teach mankind something new.

as a film script. Sumit Mitra, the *India Today* correspondent in Calcutta, knew vaguely about *The Alien*, and rang up after reading the present story to ask if that was the one I wanted to film. I said no, and gave him a brief account of what happened with *The Alien*. I was therefore very surprised to read the report in *India Today*.

Of course, there is more than the germ of a film in the present story, but this applies to most of the science fantasies I have written in the past several years.

Just now I have to make up my mind about the BBC offer before I decide on anything else. *Hirak*[28] will take another month and a half to finish. BBC wants a film on the Raj period—preferably the time of the takeover. I have ideas on it and somehow don't feel inspired; though the money and the freedom promised are tempting enough. I am in a peculiar state of mind where I find that the more the working conditions here deteriorate, the more challenging I find it. I have got so used to things not being laid out for me that I may actually find it unsettling to work in circumstances of ease and plenty. This may sound perverse, but that is how it is.

Perhaps you will come down to Bangalore during the festival when we could have a fine leisurely chat on future projects.

Yours ever,

Manik-da

---

28. *Hirak Rajar Deshe* (*The Kingdom of Diamonds*, 1980), a film Satyajit Ray was working on at the time.

15/3/82

Dear Suresh,

I'm sorry for my long silence: There have been problems with *Ghare-Baire*,[29] which needed to be sorted out. We start shooting on 5 April.

There are no plans of reviving *The Alien*. In fact, the project is all but abandoned.

The incredibly hostile and stupid reaction to *Sadgati*[30] in Bombay has put me off from Hindi films for the time being—although my faith in *Beej*[31] remains unshaken.

I'm likely to be wholly wrapped up in GB (*Ghare-Baire*) over the next four months or so, and will think of what to do next only after that.

I hope your present undertaking is making a smooth progress.

Ever yours,

Manik-da

---

29. Ray's film *The Home and the World* (1984).

30. *Sadgati* (*Deliverance*, 1981), Ray's film based on a story by Munshi Premchand, the writer of *Shatranj Ke Khilari*.

31. A short novel by Bengali writer Mahasweta Devi. Ray and I had agreed to adapt *Beej* for a film.

12/4/82

Dear Suresh,

Kamleshwar[32] was here yesterday to say they were planning to show *Sadgati* on TV towards the end of this month. They want to make it a double bill with *Shatranj* and asked me to put in a word to you. I hope there will be no problem with this.

The shooting of *Ghare-Baire* has been postponed by 7 months. Doordarshan has asked me to do another short Hindi feature. I'm interested because it will serve as a companion piece to *Sadgati* and I could then exercise my right to exploit the two together commercially.

I hope your film[33] is making good progress.

Best wishes.

Yours,

Manik-da

19 April '82

Dear Suresh,

Doordarshan is upset that you should ask 2 lakhs for *Shatranj* for TV. They say that even normally you should

---

32. A well-known Hindi literary figure. At the time, Kamleshwar was also the additional director general of Doordarshan, India's national TV channel.

33. *Katha,* a film produced by me and directed by Sai Paranjpye. It won the National Award for Best Hindi Film.

be getting well over a lakh. I have been asked to put in a word, hence this letter. I hope you will consider.

Yours,

Manik-da

26/4/82

Dear Suresh,

Who was responsible for providing Doordarshan with the atrocious Hindi-dubbed version of *Shatranj*? For me it was a nerve-shattering experience. Also, the print doesn't have the cuts I had made in the final version. The sooner this version is taken out of circulation the better. It can do nothing but incalculable harm to whatever reputation the film has acquired.

Yours,

Manik-da

21 December '83

Dear Suresh,

Thanks for your letter. I got back from the nursing home[34] about a fortnight ago and am staying at Gopa's[35] place to avoid callers and phone calls. I expect to be

---

34. After his two heart attacks.

35. Gopa Ghoshal, Mrs Ray's niece. Ray sometimes stayed with her family.

back home in a week's time. Needless to say, I'm fully recovered.

I got a letter from Costa-Gavras, who is the president of the Cinémathèque,[36] concerning the negative and the print of *Shatranj*. I have asked him to get in touch with you.

All the best.

Yours,

Manik-da

30 Aug 1985

My dear Manik-da,

I am unable to come to Calcutta this week, as the work I am involved in has got delayed. Some meetings I must have before leaving Delhi have not yet materialized.

The enclosed report is for your kind information. I will be obliged if you could find some time to go through it, and consider your and Sandip's participation in the project[37]—should it materialize. In any case, I shall be grateful for your comments and views on the report.

I will be coming to Calcutta during the latter part of next week.

With warm regards,

Sincerely,

Suresh

36. Cinémathèque Française. It has the world's most extensive film archives.

37. A Dutch project involving a dozen international directors to make a dozen short films.

P.S. In case you could participate in the project, the whole concept of getting 'a dozen directors' will be dropped.

30 Nov 1985

My dear Manik-da,

I shudder to think how pained you must be to learn that, yet again, the para-dubbed print of *Shatranj Ke Khilari* was telecast.

Enclosed herein is my letter to Doordarshan, which should explain my side. The print I gave them for the last telecast was checked and re-checked by me. The same was also seen by the art historian Dr Geeti Sen in Delhi, and she too can confirm that it was the original version and an excellent print.

I just hope you will understand that there was no negligence on my part and every possible care was taken by me.

With warm regards,
Suresh

~

Manik-da and I continued to be in touch throughout the remaining years of his life, by phone, by letter, at film festivals and during my visits to Calcutta. Our relationship remained as warm and friendly as it had been at the beginning, and thereafter, most of the time. As the years passed, we discussed future projects together, one of which was a film based on Mahasweta Devi's *Beej*. Unfortunately, after his heart attack he was not permitted by his doctors to shoot away from Calcutta, so this project (requiring extensive location shooting) did not come to fruition. There was also another film we talked seriously about making, in which the legendary Amitabh Bachchan had expressed interest in starring, but which also, most unfortunately, fell through due to an unforeseen betrayal by someone close to both of us.

10

Looking Back

♟♟♟♟♟

Stolen glances at him during pensive moments, in taxis and economy-class airplane seats, would reveal a solitary figure weighed down by the fatigue of anxiety-filled days, but with the regal bearing of one accepting it with equanimity. I saw him alternately as the 'boy standing on the burning deck' of the decaying ship that was Bengal and as a heroic Prometheus holding on to a flaming torch.

Bengal was once the glory of the Indian enlightenment. It gave India reformers such as Raja Ram Mohan Roy, Ishwar Chandra Vidyasagar, the Tagores; maharishis such as Ramakrishna Paramhansa, Swami Vivekananda and Sri Aurobindo; and militant patriots like Subhas Chandra Bose. Bengal was the political and financial capital of British India and the heart of its economic wealth. It was the luminosity of the 'jewel of the crown', now gone to seed, the burden of keeping alive its erstwhile greatness falling upon the shoulders of its one remaining giant, Satyajit Ray, through tales that would live on in moving form, documenting the places and the people he loved.

But it wasn't just Bengal Ray wanted to capture and portray. In fact, he was quite keen to explore and record every part of the country. He enjoyed filming in Varanasi and Rajasthan. In his childhood, he spent his summer holidays with his uncle in Lucknow, and carried happy memories of those days. I could see that he loved being there for the research on our film. He enjoyed it when people from the cinema world, national and international writers, and intellectuals would come to meet him and their worlds would collide. It seemed to delight him to find out what was happening in other parts of the world, especially in cinema. He would ask me if I had seen films by Adoor Gopalakrishnan, Govind Nihalani or Ketan Mehta, as though he were asking about the weather or a local deli. I was forever spinning on my heels trying to keep up with his wealth of knowledge about film and film-makers.

Due to his non-participation in social and political events, his inherent shyness, and need for time alone to create so prolifically, he was often seen as arrogant and aloof, as well as apolitical, and therefore not committed to social change. He was different from the average public or political figure in India, since he did not spout 'progressive' slogans as mere lip service in public. For him, the pursuit of excellence and creativity demanded solitude. It was a mystery to him how his attendance at a ministerial dinner was more beneficial for creativity or humanity than working intently in his study or filming somewhere.

There were many aspirants for Satyajit Ray's crown. Pygmies and their guerrillas hounded and harassed him, accusing him of everything under the sun, hoping to gain fame by dragging him down. He kept a stoic silence against their diatribes and continued with his work.

I was in awe of the man and the admiration has only grown stronger since his passing. He was, and remains, the most important of my many great teachers in this lifetime. I realized that being with Satyajit Ray was the same as being in a gurukul, where only complete surrender by the shishya is the path to attain the teacher's affection and wisdom. Even when we had our disagreements, and our one serious falling out, Manik-da never withdrew his love and I refused to revoke my faith and devotion.

Satyajit Ray led a modest life. Between his family, a dozen or so close friends, his team of superb technicians and his prodigious creativity, he neither needed nor wanted any other life than the simple but highly creative one he chose to live.

Most people were overawed by the sheer magnificence

of his personality and achievements; thus, the enormous dignity that was a natural part of him was often construed to be vanity and snobbishness, which was far from the truth. One often heard him on the phone trying to dissuade someone from coming to visit him, but if the caller persisted, he never refused to see them, with the rider, 'OK, but just for fifteen minutes.' Once they were there, he would never ask visitors to leave or make them feel unwelcome.

Manik-da had serious heart and blood pressure problems for years, and like me, he was a chain smoker, which didn't help his condition. One of the reasons he gave me for continuing to smoke was: 'Baba, this pressure from people is so difficult. It is always "Please, Manik-da, just for fifteen minutes", or "So and so will be upset if you don't come, Manik-da". Now that the doctors have told me I absolutely must be firm in stopping this, I feel enormous relief.' But despite his natural reticence and need for privacy, his door was never closed to struggling film-makers, novelists, scholars, or anybody else who wanted to benefit humanity in some way.

It always embarrassed him to be seen as getting any sort of special treatment. Throughout his career, he often had to fly, and because he was tall he needed a lot of legroom. Getting the right seat was important, so he was always the first person to arrive at an airport. This used to upset me terribly. 'But, Manik-da, the airline should understand that you are an exceptionally tall person and provide you a decent seat in advance ... besides, you're not just anybody. You are Satyajit Ray! I am going to call the airline.'

'No, Baba. I don't mind getting to the airport early. We can always chat and read there.'

Usually the first one in line at the check-in counter, he would come back enormously pleased that he had got the seat of his choice, almost like a child who stood first in his class. That is the picture of him that stays with me and brings a smile even now.

Like all unaware and egoistic students, I never realized until much later how deeply his behaviour, words and ideas had embedded themselves into my psyche. He was always surprised that others could not achieve what he had or didn't have the sensitivity and genius that he had.

'Manik-da, how can one learn to operate the camera?' I asked one day, amazed by his proficiency in handling it.

'Suresh, cameramen just mystify the whole thing. You only have to know what image you want to capture. You are an engineer, surely you can figure out the optic details of light and image?'

He never made anyone feel as though they were in the presence of a creative and intellectual genius. He encouraged me and everyone else to do everything he did by making it seem so simple.

As far as his professional behaviour was concerned,

Ray was honest and respectful. Whether it was a decision regarding salary, arrangements for locations, hotels or matters relating to film distribution, he never interfered in my work as a producer. He always wanted, through his films, to return the producers' money, although he was acutely aware that his films had a limited audience. I have never met a more practical film-maker than him, nor have I seen or heard of a director more considerate towards his producers in my twenty-five years in cinema. He was hurt more than anyone at the waste of our money. Long after our films were done, if we ever needed his help in solving problems, he was always available and willing. Those of us who were fortunate enough to be his producers are still enjoying the benefits of his creations. Riding on his coattails, we get to be at least a footnote in the history of cinema.

~

On a personal level, his Bengali roots were deep. He was in love with Calcutta: where he was born and where he took his last breath.

More than once he told me, 'Suresh, I have to make one film a year to give work to my unit. A lot of them have been with me from the beginning.' He also used to say that to make a good film it is very important to be understanding and to have patience with other people's faults. If someone working on his film did not fulfil his or her responsibility, instead of getting angry he would simply do the task himself. Given my sudden angry outbursts at what I perceived to be incompetence or irresponsibility, these were important lessons.

I was also amazed by Ray's extraordinary creative energy which resulted in the continuous stream of films, screenplays, novels, short stories, music, paintings, graphics, set design and even the music and posters for his films. Apart from this, he would undertake endless research for each film, after which he would visit local houses, shops, temples, museums and places of interest. He always answered all his correspondence personally, either by hand or on a portable typewriter balanced precariously on his gangly knees. He also answered his own phone, opened the door for his guests, read voraciously and watched sports avidly on television, hardly ever missing an important football, cricket or tennis match. I often wondered how he found the time for all this! Throughout the time I knew him, he was always working intensely on something and his self-discipline was unparalleled. Manik-da seemed to view relaxation as an avoidable foe.

He lived a complete life in samsara and relished life immensely, although seemingly aware of its impermanence. My friend Neelam Mukherji surprised me when she gave me his copy of the Bhagavad Gita, which he had presented her with after she had suffered a heart attack. I hadn't realized the depth of his spirituality since film had always been our main connection.

After his heart attack and bypass surgery in Houston, it was a long time before the doctors allowed him to make films again. When he was finally given the go-ahead, he was as happy as a child. 'Suresh, at last the doctors have agreed with me that I actually *do* stay calm while directing a film, so there's no reason not to let me do it!'

~

'Dada, how did you learn film-making?' I inquired one day. 'By watching films,' he answered instantaneously. 'And, Suresh, you must see all the *bad* films of the *good* film directors. That is how you will learn from their mistakes.'

While working on my first film I heard a legend about Ray from our director Basu Chatterjee. When Ray was sent for training to the London head office of the advertising firm of which he was the creative director in Calcutta, he watched almost hundred films in his three months there. And before he went to see a film based on a literary classic, he would write his own screenplay and compare it to what he later saw. There was nothing in the world of cinema that he didn't seem to know. He was a veritable encyclopaedia on the topic. He never refused to see films by struggling film-makers. At film festivals, he and Sandip usually saw three to four films a day!

Ray was not only a brilliant creator of films, he was a symbol of the aspirations and the possibilities of every Indian of his era seeking to make it on the international stage. Now, in an era when Indian beauty queens, film-makers, authors who write in English, doctors and scientists have made it big globally; when *Slumdog Millionaire* won the Oscar for best film of the year in 2009; and lakhs of Indian tech wizards advise the world every day on its technical glitches; it is hard to understand how impossible it was for a 'Third World' artist to make it in the racist, white-dominated film world of the 1950s and 1960s, when most of the world was still under the shackles of colonialism. Back then, to be asked if we had seen a telephone was a normal and polite query, and entering an upscale establishment without the company of a white friend was daunting. And it was not just in South Africa or Rhodesia that a brown person couldn't go to the same restroom as his white friends, but even in the southern states of the so-called 'democratic' United States. Even in liberal Los Angeles, landladies would hurriedly tell you that the apartment had *just* been rented, even though the FOR RENT sign belied their words. Reservation agents at airlines would make you wait until they had attended to every white customer, even though you were ahead in the queue. Young Cockney-accented immigration officials would barrage you with the most humiliating and inane questions when you were ferried from Dover (UK) to Calais (France), even though you were an American green card holder. It was an era when the only blacks to be found on Hollywood and British screens were the ones playing drug addicts and prostitutes, murderers and rapists, soul singers and jazz musicians, domestic staff and plantation workers mumbling, 'Yes, bwana', 'Yes, massa'.

Even Ray had run-ins of this sort early on in his international career. When he was invited to be on the jury of the Cannes Film Festival, only one invite was sent to him. Never one to ask for anything, he inquired if he could bring his wife along, since he knew this was a matter of policy for those invited. The festival coordinator reluctantly agreed and sent him two economy-class tickets. Since economy seats were extremely uncomfortable for him, he made further enquiries and found out that the festival always sent first-class tickets along with five-star hotel accommodation, as is the norm even now. Rather than raise a fuss, he declined the invitation and didn't attend the festival.

His influence on young people in India cannot be measured. While we were on the promotional tour for *Shatranj Ke Khilari* and guests of Harvard University, I met a pretty, intelligent and bright-eyed girl at the showing of our film at the Museum of Fine Arts in Boston. She told me she was dying to meet Ray and asked if a meeting could be arranged for that evening.

I apologized and said it would not be possible since we had been invited to dinner at a university don's home and couldn't bring an extra person along. Somehow, she managed an invitation which made me happy. But she didn't even notice me. Post-dinner she spent all her time sitting on the floor at the master's feet, gazing at him with adoration. Mira Nair later told me: 'Suresh, it was *that* evening that I decided to risk becoming a film-maker ... I realized that it was possible for us Indians to make it on the international scene.' And Mira has done well in expanding the dream that Ray began. She went on to become an accomplished and recognized director, writer and producer, with her own film company, Mirabai Films, making international hits such as *Salaam Bombay* and *Monsoon Wedding*.

~

Having made thirty films of exceptional quality and despite his status as an icon of cinema and an international celebrity, Ray continued to live in a rented apartment. His widow, Bijoya Ray, lived in that apartment till her death in 2015. Sandip continues to live there. His films, though always deep and meaningful, never had huge audiences in India, where the trend has always been escapist Hindi musicals. Internationally, although highly regarded, his films played mainly to audiences that attended small art cinemas. Thus, he never earned enough to live the high life that other much-less-talented directors did.

He probably remains the most decorated Indian film-maker ever, when it comes to international awards. President Mitterrand of France personally honoured Ray with the Légion d'Honneur in Calcutta; a representative of the Academy of Motion Picture Arts and Sciences came to Belle Vue hospital in Calcutta to present him the Oscar for Lifetime Achievement while he was on his deathbed; he was given the Bharat Ratna, India's highest civilian honour; Oxford University awarded him an honorary doctorate—not to mention the top accolades won at film festivals across the world.

But these honours will not be his lasting glory. It is his films, his kindness and his humanity for which he is remembered. This was a man who never refused anyone in pursuit of a dream. I personally saw many instances of this in his lifetime. During the Emergency in India, the sycophantic puppets of the government banned Shyam Benegal's film *Nishant* from being sent to foreign film festivals. Ray and I were staying at the President Hotel in Bombay at the time. Shyam's wife, Neera, tracked me down by phone, pleading that Ray write to Indira Gandhi (the then prime minister) to allow Shyam's film to go abroad.

'Suresh, his career will be ruined if the film doesn't go. They have asked us to insert a card saying that the conditions shown in the film no longer exist in India.

Shyam has even agreed to that and still they won't let the film go. Will you please ask Manik-da to write a letter to Mrs Gandhi?'

'But, Neera, we are just about to leave for the airport.'

'Please, Suresh. I will have it picked up right away.'

'Okay, let me talk to him. I'll call you back.'

Manik-da had been listening to the conversation. 'What is it, Baba? Any problem?'

I explained the situation to him, adding, 'Neera's sister, Anjali, is married to my best friend from school, Suresh Malhotra. As a Punjabi, I can't refuse when she asks for my help. It's like family asking...'

'Suresh, is Shyam's office on the way to the airport?'

'Yes, sir.'

He immediately wrote the letter. On the way, we stopped at Shyam's office at Jyoti Studios and dropped it off. *Nishant* could now go abroad.

I remember once a senior technician asked Ray to request Doordarshan to get his relative transferred from one centre to another. Serious clout with the government was needed to accomplish something like this. Manik-da did the needful. And when James Ivory shot *The Householder*—the first film of Merchant-Ivory Productions—he appealed to Ray to help edit it. Along with Dulal Dutta, his master editor from the *Pather Panchali* days, Manik-da cheerfully obliged despite his jam-packed schedule. He wrote many synopses and reviewed many books. Whatever he was asked, and whatever he could do, he always did, willingly.

~

After he suffered two heart attacks while making *Ghare-Baire*, his son Sandip had to complete the film, following Ray's detailed instructions. Ray spent the mid-1980s in fragile health. He did not film at all for about four years. After that he made three more films, which were a departure from his earlier ones.

The last time I saw him, before his final hospitalization, his parting words, as he led me to the door, were: 'And, Baba, one more thing—just keep working.'

I nodded my head in agreement because I knew that that was his elixir, and out of compassion he wanted me to have the same. I was racked with guilt—because despite my promise I knew I didn't possess half his stamina—and deep sorrow, because he was sick and I couldn't bear the thought of losing him. But when I looked into his eyes, all else faded away except for an overwhelming gratitude.

Satyajit Ray, my very dear Manik-da, died on 23 April 1992, and I can say, in all honesty, that some of my dreams, my film ideals and a part of my life died with him. But after a long period of desolation, I found that an eternal gratitude had replaced the pain his parting had caused. And this gratitude I will carry with me to future lifetimes, where I hope with all my heart we may meet and work together again.

Acknowledgements

It is always difficult to remember all those who made a book possible.

First, I would like to thank my late friend Pranab Basu to whom I first mooted the idea with a request to read the letters. He not only confirmed my intuition that the letters could make the backbone of a book but also actively encouraged me to start the writing.

I have to admire Dechen Pradhan, who with great patience and care typed the handwritten letters, numbered them and collated them by date.

After struggling with a few drafts, I finally sat with my friend Emeshe Williams, fellow student at UCLA, to do the final draft, which she herself typed. She jogged my memory for events and incidents I had forgotten, and also asked me crucial questions to identify the different Indian personalities in the text and include their details in the footnotes. We easily assume that others worldwide are as familiar with us as we are in India, which of course is not so.

At length, I finally gathered the courage to show it to professional writers. Jean-Claude Carrière was the first one and he generously agreed to write the superb foreword. In India my long-time friend Tavleen Singh was the first to see the manuscript. It was her encouragement and praise that made me show the manuscript to others.

I am deeply grateful to Premola Ghosh and Indrani Majumdar at the India International Centre, who vetted the manuscript further. Indrani's expertise as a Ray scholar was of immense help in correcting factual errors and dates.

I am grateful to Madhu Jain for connecting me with Mona Joshi, who edited the book before it went to the publishers. Mona did a Herculean job, with extreme care and precision.

My heartfelt thanks to Richard Gere for taking time out from his crowded schedule to read the book and write a blurb for it.

Without Sathya Saran, this book would not have reached HarperCollins. It was a chance meeting with her at the Lucknow Literary Festival that reconnected us and that prompted her to take up the promotion of the book.

Of course, without the applied and concentrated dedication of Shantanu Ray Chaudhuri at HarperCollins, the book would not have seen its final form.

A word of gratitude and thanks to Andrew Robinson, for his wonderful introduction to the book and his enthusiasm for it.

Finally, I must thank my domestic staff, Geetaram Painully and Chander Sharma, who bear my irritations and moods to keep me comfortable and in good health.

I sincerely apologize for any names I may have inadvertently left out.

25 ▪ HarperCollins India Ltd

Celebrating 25 Years of Great Publishing

HarperCollins India celebrates its twenty-fifth anniversary in 2017. Twenty-five years of publishing India's finest writers and some of its most memorable books – those you cannot put down; ones you want to finish reading yet don't want to end; works you can read over and over again only to fall deeper in love with.

Through the years, we have published writers from the Indian subcontinent, and across the globe, including Aravind Adiga, Kiran Nagarkar, Amitav Ghosh, Jhumpa Lahiri, Manu Joseph, Anuja Chauhan, Upamanyu Chatterjee, A.P.J. Abdul Kalam, Shekhar Gupta, M.J. Akbar, Satyajit Ray, Gulzar, Surender Mohan Pathak and Anita Nair, amongst others, with approximately 200 new books every year and an active print and digital catalogue of more than 1,000 titles, across ten imprints. Publishing works of various genres including literary fiction, poetry, mind body spirit, commercial fiction, journalism, business, self-help, cinema, biographies – all with attention to quality, of the manuscript and the finished product – it comes as no surprise that we have won every major literary award including the Man Booker Prize, the Sahitya Akademi Award, the DSC Prize, the Hindu Literary Prize, the MAMI Award for Best Writing on Cinema, the National Award for Best Book on Cinema, the Crossword Book Award, and the Publisher of the Year, twice, at Publishing Next in Goa and, in 2016, at Tata Literature Live, Mumbai.

We credit our success to the people who make us who we are, and will be celebrating this anniversary with: our authors, retailers, partners, readers and colleagues at HarperCollins India. Over the years, a firm belief in our promise and our passion to deliver only the very best of the printed word has helped us become one of India's finest in publishing. Every day we endeavour to deliver bigger and better – for you.

Thank you for your continued support and patronage.

HarperCollins*Publishers*India

🐦 @HarperCollinsIN

📷 @HarperCollinsIN

📘 @HarperCollinsIN

💼 HarperCollins Publishers India

www.harpercollins.co.in

Harper Broadcast

Showcasing celebrated authors, book reviews, plot trailers, cover reveals, launches and interviews, Harper Broadcast is live and available for free subscription on the brand's social media channels through a new newsletter. Hosted by renowned TV anchor and author Amrita Tripathi, Broadcast is a snapshot of all that is news, views, extracts, sneak peeks and opinions on books. Tune in to conversations with authors, where we get up close and personal about their books, why they write and what's coming up.

Harper Broadcast is the first of its kind in India, a publisher-hosted news channel for all things publishing within HarperCollins. Follow us on Twitter and YouTube.

Subscribe to the monthly newsletter here: https://harpercollins.co.in/newsletter/

📺 Harper Broadcast

🐦 @harperbroadcast

www.harperbroadcast.com

Address

HarperCollins Publishers India Ltd
A-75, Sector 57, Noida, UP 201301, India

Phone
+91-120-4044800